The Whole Cure

52 Essential Prescriptions to Overcome Overwhelm, Reclaim Balance and Reconnect with a Life You Love!

Dr. Jennifer L. Weinberg, MD, MPH, MBE

The Whole Cure: 52 Essential Prescriptions to Overcome Overwhelm, Reclaim Balance and Reconnect with a Life You Love!

To contact the author, visit www.JenniferWeinbergMD.com

Printed in the United States of America

ISBN-13: 978-1501089213

ISBN-10: 1501089218

First Edition

To my loving and supportive family, mentors and guides. Thank you for inspiring my light to shine by selflessly sharing your light and generosity. Love and gratitude for your understanding, inspiration and unfailing encouragement!

CONTENTS

INTRODUCTION: Embracing the Whole Cure

MANY OF US ARE SO BUSY and rush about our daily lives. We can become caught up in the daily grind, overwhelmed, burned out, anxious and stressed! Our modern society is so focused on working harder and longer, acquiring possessions and achieving titles that we often forget about and lose touch with our true nature—that wise, beautiful, loving and vibrant being within each of us.

As a highly-sensitive individual and perfectionist, I am all too familiar with the intensity and consequences of living life as a constant battle. For too many years, I pushed on and ignored the wisdom my body and soul were trying to send me. I worked harder, longer and more intensely. I earned one more degree, worked out one hour longer, took on one more project and said "yes" to one more request that did not align with my true passions. The idea that I could take time to simply be present and enjoy a moment without being "productive" was unacceptable despite my body's screams for rest, relaxation and simply space to breathe.

I knew that health required balance and even taught my patients about this crucial concept, yet I was constantly depleted. No matter how much I exercised, ate a balanced whole-foods diet, slept longer or took trendy vitamins or supplements, I constantly felt exhausted, run-down and unsettled.

Even when drained and overwhelmed, I failed to give myself permission to take a break. I succumbed to the pressure to take the traditional path and follow the steps that I believed were expected of me. I felt an unsettling stirring inside of me yet suppressed that wise voice of truth that knew my real path. I was depleted. Depleted of energy, passion for life and genuine purpose as I strayed farther from my authentic path.

If you can relate to this sense of exhaustion and lack of authentic fulfillment, then I hope that these inspirational concepts and powerful prescriptions will free you from the relentless cycle of driving yourself to depletion as they have for me and so many of my patients and clients. I invite you to embrace *The Whole Cure*. Give yourself permission to transform the challenges of everyday life, and realign your body, mind and lifestyle with self-care, gratitude and mindfulness.

As you shift your mindset to make yourself your own priority, you will go from depletion to fulfillment. You will notice miraculous shifts in your thoughts, words, actions and energy. As you work through my clear yet awe-inspiring prescriptions, you will uncover what has been holding you back from truly having the vibrant, healthy, balanced body and life that you have always wanted.

The Whole Cure provides a wonderful starting point for embracing the opportunity to become more present, calm, relaxed and reflective. Each chapter introduces a core inspirational concept which is crucial to vibrant health and a fulfilled, authentic and balanced life. Exemplifying these concepts, my associated prescriptions provide an action plan to guide you in cultivating balance, nourishing your best self, unlocking your potential and achieving enhanced mindfulness. Each practical prescription takes only a few moments to read and begin to implement but has profound and long-lasting impacts on your health and wellbeing. I offer inspirational strategies for releasing fear, cultivating mindfulness, allowing gratitude, finding forgiveness and inviting love to flow towards yourself and others.

Each prescription will help you release blockages, reconnect with your innate wisdom and move forward to fully live your inspired life. You will flourish as you shatter unhealthy assumptions, recognize your value and trust in the magnificent wisdom you hold within you. You will learn to adopt a new mindset that leaves you fulfilled, at peace and transformed. Choosing loving thoughts over delusional fears, asserting your truth instead of giving over your power and releasing destructive patterns to recalibrate your life will become second nature as you dedicate yourself to living a vibrant authentic life.

When you are able to reconnect with this authentic self, you can act out of a place of alignment with your purpose. This leads you to feel strong, confident, vibrant and whole as you act in accordance with your life purpose and true passions. You can reconnect with your whole spirit and live your life with vibrancy and true passion as you follow a path that is authentic and not one you think you should or must follow.

Connecting with this whole spirit within you provides peace and a sense that life is flowing as it should. Anxiety, depression and worry melt away. Physical suffering is lifted. You are energized as you embrace the amazing being which you are and act from a place of authenticity and alignment.

How to Get the Most Out of This Experience

I have hand-picked these fifty-two proven prescriptions to offer you simple yet powerful techniques. As you engage in the material and exercises, you will be inspired to reconnect with your inner wisdom and uncover enhanced inner strength and peace. You will find yourself able to overcome the most taxing challenges of daily life—disconnect, stress, overwhelm, burnout, frustration, resentment and lack of fulfillment. You will be able to immediately implement these transformational principles in your life. This guide is designed so that you can achieve peace, balance, energy and a connection with your true passion now!

Inspired by great spiritual teachings and the best of lifestyle science, these practical, powerful, easy to implement tools will empower you to live with greater ease and reclaim your true self. These inspirational prescriptions encompass life-changing principles, presented as easy-to-implement techniques. As you practice these skills in your day-to-day life, you will deepen your connection to your inner strength, overcome overwhelm, melt away fears and settle into a place of peace. *The Whole Cure* provides profound strategies to allow you to become more conscientious, confident, peaceful, relaxed and revitalized! As you cultivate balance, gratitude and mindfulness, you are inspired and energized to create and live the life of your heartfelt desires!

This practical guide emphasizes exercises that will help you reconnect with your true passions, decrease anxiety and celebrate life! These fifty-two prescriptions will support you in overcoming overwhelm, reclaiming balance and reconnecting with a life you love. The book is designed to be flexible and work within your life. You can choose to engage in each exercise at your own pace or dedicate yourself to exploring one topic each month. Each prescription can be embraced as a living meditation for a one week or longer period, during which you can reflect on the topic for that chapter and the specific challenge presented in the prescription for that week. Feel free to listen to your intuition and allow it to guide you.

I invite you to engage in these prescriptions and strategies to open up greater possibilities and lead you to a more fulfilling and peaceful life. With each step you take, you are empowered to access your authentic core values and natural state of radiance! This brilliance, natural guidance, grounded peace, serenity, prosperity and love reside within you. As you open up your awareness, quiet your mind and cultivate your ability to live in accordance with your authentic self, these qualities thrive, and you cultivate the health and life you have always wanted.

Simply Whole Prescriptions: Warning—may cause profound and powerful shifts in your life, health, relationships and perspective!

Dedicating just a few minutes of your day to reflect on and implement these simple proven strategies will powerfully change your life! Building your Simple Pure Whole™ toolkit will ultimately lead to a breathtaking experience of life filled with abundance, acceptance, joy, balance and appreciation. If you fulfill these prescriptions, you can expect incredible transformation simply by adding up subtle shifts to create profound change.

You can change your patterns, habits, health and life when you are dedicated to shifting your perspective, letting go of your fears and opening your heart, mind and energy to be guided to new possibilities and perspectives. This guidance comes in many forms when we are ready and open to receiving it. *The Whole Cure* helps you create a life in which you can experience intuition, inspiration and synchronicities that steer you towards the right path for you. Listen deeply and with curiosity to your inner spirit. In those moments when your thoughts and actions are aligned with love, you are led to inspiration. When you are in touch with the flow of the universe, you live from a place of strength and truth. Fundamentally, recognizing your inherent inner knowledge provides you with invaluable gifts.

As you live a more aligned life, cultivate mindfulness and practice gratitude, these moments become more frequent, and your life is full of abundance, acceptance and appreciation. The prescriptions in *The Whole Cure* will guide you in shifting your perspective and transforming your mindset and life. The more you choose mindfulness, gratitude, love and authenticity, the more miraculous transformation occurs. Your life, health and relationships shift and feel grounded, at peace and moving in the right direction.

Your energy has immense power. There is energy in your presence, your thoughts, your words and your actions. When we live from a place of fear, stress, overwhelm, inauthenticity or chaos, our thoughts, words, actions and energy can negatively impact the world around us and attract situations which are not optimal. However when we are mindful of our presence and energy in the world and function from a place of gratitude, positivity and self-assurance, the world we live in becomes more in sync with our purpose. Life flows more easily. We are more in tune with natural cycles around us. When we take responsibility for our own energy, we help dissolve boundaries and blockages and let in love. As life flows effortlessly, we gain greater creativity, energy and productivity with less effort. You have the power to awaken and elevate the energy you bring into the world!

Start today with these practical yet transformational tools to allow you to shatter through your stresses and blocks so you can change your patterns and discover what makes you truly blissful, balanced and healthy. I am excited for you to start overcoming overwhelm, reclaiming balance and reconnecting with your authentic life! As you awaken to your own inner light and strength, you cultivate a powerful presence that enlightens the world around you as well. I invite you to live a life which embraces and reflects your greatest potential, filled with vibrant health, abundance, true joy, passion and meaning. Your authentic presence is powerful!

CHAPTER 1: Living From Passionate Purpose and Creativity

AS WE GROW UP AND TAKE ON more and more responsibilities and burdens we often get caught up in the busyness of everyday life. We can go faster and do more and more yet feel like we are no closer to achieving our dreams than we were weeks or even years ago. Daily tasks can become overwhelming when we are disconnected from ourselves, our communities and our passions. We can lose our sense of magic, imagination, joy and wonder. Our lives can be crammed with to-dos but begin to lack a sense of purpose.

Are you passionate about what you do every day? Each of us possesses a purpose and unique talents which help us fulfil that purpose. When you are using these talents and are passionate about what you are doing, you are more engaged and rejuvenated. When you find those things about which you are truly passionate, they feel natural and energizing. Being excited about what you do each day allows you to more fully share your gifts with the world in a way that is truly fulfilling.

Living in this type of alignment also cultivates energy. Passion *is* energy. When you live from a place of passionate enthusiasm, you cultivate a positive energy that fills you up and radiates out from you into the world. Connecting with your passions can also help you tap into a state of flow. In this zone, time seems to stand still and everything flows naturally and with ease. You become more focused and experience joy, enthusiasm and full immersion.

Purpose

When you are aligned with your genuine essence and live in congruence with your authentic purpose and passions, the world opens up to you in magical and uplifting ways. Open your heart, mind and spirit and you can listen, feel and engage in the wisdom that is within you. As you begin to listen to and trust your intuition more fully, you can connect with your passions and rediscover your unique life purpose.

"The two most important days in your life are the day you are born and the day you find out why."
-Mark Twain

Each of us has a unique and profound reason for being here. When you uncover and remember this intelligence, you step into your place in the world and can allow your brilliant light to shine forth! Consistently living your life to the fullest with meaning, purpose, happiness and fulfillment, allows your confidence to soar and leads you to approach your life with appreciation and passion. Live in harmony with your purpose, and your life shifts in profound ways.

Each moment you have a choice to create the energy of your life with your thoughts, words and actions. We decide where and how to direct our energy. This empowers you to create a life you truly love. Given the immense influence you have over your life, it is so important to gain clarity about what you truly want to create and experience. Use the prescriptions in this chapter to explore what you sincerely want in life and what you are doing to create that.

Emotional Intelligence

Often even very smart people can make terrible decisions. The problem arises when they act from a reactionary place and are not grounded and connected to their inner wisdom and strength. Emotions are complex and involved in every aspect of our lives from relationships to learning. The ways in which we react to, regulate and interact with our emotions has profound repercussions for how we navigate our lives.

To align with your purpose and live life with passion, one thing you can do is cultivate your emotional intelligence. The way you manage your emotions and interact with others can greatly impact your success and happiness. Your emotional intelligence refers to the way you manage your own and others emotions. This critical trait involves self-regulation, self-awareness, social skills, motivation and empathy. People with greater emotional intelligence are better able to work towards goals, remain adaptable, recover from stress and exhibit confidence. Rather than ignoring them or misinterpreting them, emotionally-intelligent people are able to recognize emotions when they arise, take a step back, recognize what they are feeling and examine how those emotions are impacting their experiences, thoughts and behaviors.

Self-Expression and Creativity

Self-expression is an integral component of connecting with and cultivating your emotional intelligence and true passionate purpose. We all have talents and gifts which we can use to express and share our inner spirits. The way you express yourself is a reflection of the way you approach and interpret the world and your place in it. When you use the energy of communication and creative expression to authentically give of yourself, you can share your unique gifts, talents and light with the world. Allowing your creativity to shine can help you to cultivate your passions and build an authentic, balanced life.

Sometimes it can feel scary to bare your soul. You may feel exposed and vulnerable at first, but openly expressing your voice and giving fully of your creativity and talents allows you to authentically communicate your essential truth. When you are living from a place of fear, negativity, judgment and overwhelm, the energy you put forth will reflect those negative emotions. Instead of holding back your potential, focus on allowing the energy of communication and creative expression to flow easily in your life. To freely and fully express your truth in a positive and life-affirming way, you need to acknowledge and shift these old emotional patterns.

As you align with the free flow of creativity, you will be able to access a transformational way of expressing your core truth, through voice, behavior and even quiet presence. When you access this place of truth and authentic expression, you begin to speak with your vibrant inner voice. This truth is aligned with your soul and speaks clearly and avidly from a place of courage and passion instead of trying to blindly comply, align with outside pressures or please others. When communication arises from your core self, you are able to share your inner light with others in a simple, kind and open manner that benefits you and those around you.

> "Life is the art of drawing without an eraser."
> -John Gardner

Truth, creativity and passionate purpose are within you! You are a vibrant, unique and creative being with a valuable truth and spirit to share with the world. Connecting with your inner wisdom and true passions moves you towards living in alignment with your genuine purpose and unites you with the larger community and flow of energy of the universe. As you allow your inner spirit to shine into the world in your unique way, you embrace your authentic purpose and life flows with more ease. Finding and activating your expression is integral to living a Simply Whole™ life!

Cultivating Stillness, Passion and Purpose

Our lives are so busy and filled with noise and distractions that it can be easy to get caught up in a reactionary state, feeling overwhelmed and constantly chasing your to-do list. Yet it is amongst the chaos and busyness that it is most important to learn to slow down and create a stillness where you can listen to your inner knowing and intuition. As you open up the space to hear and trust your inner guidance, you will naturally act in greater alignment with your true purpose. And in turn, you will create positivity, passion, creativity, flow and ease in your life!

This is the way to break free from the struggle and settle into the peace that comes when you focus on what truly matters instead of the material distractions that are all around us. Stepping into your power to live in alignment with your heart instead of following outside messages about what you think you "should" do, opens up true possibilities and a profound energy, ease and flow. You begin to make choices that are aligned with your heart's passions and put forth effort into the world that is truly meaningful. This allows you to live out your purpose each day with passion, creativity and enthusiasm.

"The ability to be in the present moment is a major component of mental wellness."
- Abraham Maslow

Slow down and listen within to discover what ignites your passion. An essential channel for connecting with our passionate purpose is being in the moment. To enhance your passion and strengthen your connection to your authentic purpose, explore yourself, your core values and your deepest desires more profoundly. Taking time to reignite your sense of curiosity, fun and spontaneity can help recharge your passions and reconnect you with the magic that is all around. What inspires you to live with enthusiasm and passion? Engage in the prescriptions in this chapter to find greater clarity and move towards a life filled with passion and enthusiasm!

PRESCRIPTION: SLOW DOWN TO PEAK PASSION

Meditation can be a helpful means for reconnecting with your true passions and rediscovering your authentic calling. The simple act of slowing down, quieting the mind and going inward can help you develop your ability to be present. In turn, this can strengthen your connection to your authentic purpose and give you a clearer sense of passionate devotion. Try this simple meditative practice to enhance your mindfulness and bring yourself more fully into the present moment.

Choose a task, thought or experience you have recently had in your life, and write about it on a piece of paper. Alternatively, you can choose a simple everyday object like a flower or vegetable on which to focus. Place the paper or object aside, out of view.

Sit comfortably and close your eyes. Breathe deeply and with ease. Allow your thoughts to just be, without trying to control or change them. Allow both the breath and your thoughts to come and go, flowing freely. When you are ready, bring your attention to your heart. Feel your heart filled with light, love and passion. With each inhale imagine a positive energy building and filling you up. Sit quietly, and sense this positive flow of energy for a few minutes.

When you are ready, slowly bring your awareness back to the present moment and space. Open your eyes and gradually return your senses to your environment. Retrieve the paper or object you chose earlier.

Contemplate the task, experience, thought or object. With enhanced awareness, take a closer look at this target. What about it grabs your attention? Where can you find beauty in your target? What is unique about how you now interpret it? Look more deeply, and notice what arises in your awareness. Think about the past, present and future of the experience, thought or object. Journal about what you notice.

You may note that you have a deeper sense of observation or a more complete perception of your target after the meditative experience of cultivating your inner presence. How can you continue to foster this awareness in your life? What can this simple yet profound practice bring to your daily activities if you repeat it daily or several times throughout your day? Imagine what you can experience in your day-to-day life when you cultivate such increased depth and awareness of yourself and your experiences.

Use this enhanced understanding to connect more deeply with your passions and better understand your purpose. Bring this heightened mindfulness into your interactions, work, relationships and actions. Cultivate an increased presence, and allow it to guide your journey inward. Notice how this changes your experiences and reignites your passion and energy!

PRESCRIPTION: UNCOVERING YOUR NATURAL PASSIONS

Identify Your Targets: One of the first steps on the path to living in alignment with your authentic purpose is to identify that which truly resonates with your soul. Take some time to reflect upon and journal about the following questions.

- When was the last time you felt true joy? What were you doing? Who were you with? In what setting were you?
- What people, places, activities, things, experiences and atmospheres bring you joy, make you feel energized and give you a sense of true purpose?
- What people, places, activities, things, experiences and atmospheres make you feel angry, sad, guilty or bored? What experiences fill you with a sense of dread and overwhelm?
- What situations, people, atmospheres and activities make you feel like everything is right, balanced and flowing just the way it needs to in your life? How do you feel when you experience this energy?
- What values, emotions and energy do you want to foster, reflect and emanate into the world?
- How can you cultivate an atmosphere and energy of growth, learning, exploration and creation in your life?

Connect with Your Flow: Sit down and allow yourself to just write. Take a few deep breaths, quiet your mind and let the words flow through you onto the paper. Relax into whatever you feel drawn to write—a story, a poem, thoughts, feelings, a drawing or a doodle. Allow anything that comes to mind to flow onto the paper.

Open Your Mind and Notice: Go through your day with an open mind to notice the world and your environment. Take note of "signs" around you. What speaks to you? Is there something that catches your attention? Let the universe call to you and listen. Perhaps a song comes on the radio at just the right time or you see a literal sign on a billboard? Maybe you meet someone who happens to have an insight or opportunity you need at just that moment?

Use these exercises to rediscover and build on your natural capabilities and awareness. Each of us has unique strengths, talents and interests. As we go through life and take on expectations and ideas of what we think we are supposed to be or how we perceive others expect us to act, we may forget these natural gifts. Notice what unfolds in your life as you uncover your natural passions!

PRESCRIPTION: PLAY PASSIONATELY

Play! Our essential true self is pure love. From this source of endless joy, stems your natural state of playfulness. Although our everyday lives can make us feel limited and trapped by an endless to-do list, a path we think we must follow or others we feel we must please, being fully alive involves letting go of these fears.

The carefree experience of play allows you to be more fully alive. Through this opening, you are able to see and experience the world in a more receptive way. With expanded possibilities, your brain can refresh, and your spirit is renewed. This lightness and carefree expression allow you to expand and open to your passionate purpose.

Reconnect with your inner child and allow yourself to play for fun! Run around a park, build a fort, make up a game, play fetch with your dog, experiment in the kitchen.

Make a list of ways that you can play and let go. Take time to go out and do something you loved to do as a child or have not done in a while. Experience what it is like to allow yourself to play, and feel free to simply enjoy yourself!

Why Not? Reflect on how it feels to be carefree and release your need to be a certain way. If you feel guilty or self-critical about taking time out of your busy life to engage in joyful play, journal about what feelings are coming forth. Why do you think you acquired those beliefs? What is holding you back from valuing playtime, down time and time to renew your spirit?

Think about the way you feel when you do engage in carefree play. What is it like for you to let go, to stop worrying about your to-do list and to take time to simply allow your soul to enjoy the experience of being alive? Incorporating a sense of play into your day-to-day life affirms your joyful spirit, spontaneity and fun. List how play helps you to be more creative, energetic, productive, renewed, joyful, refreshed and happy.

Compare the two lists you have made of the reasons you feel guilty for taking time for play and the benefits you receive when you engage in joyful play. Notice how incorporating the vibrancy of play can renew your spirit and help you feel less trapped in fear. Observe how play can lift heaviness from your heart and expand your spirit.

Rediscover Your Talents and Passions! Take some time to rediscover your inborn talents and embrace them. Look back on your childhood. What did you love to do? What activities did you lose yourself in and became so immersed in that time seemed irrelevant? What topics did you love to read about or learn about just for fun? What made you light up with passion and enthusiasm for life? Were there experiences, tasks, hobbies or pursuits that made you look at the world in a different light?

Now think about your life today. What would you spend your time doing if money were no issue? What would you choose to work on if you did not feel the need to conform to other people's standards or ideas?

Pick a book that you feel drawn to, and open it up randomly to any page. Read whatever passage your eyes fall to first. How do those words speak to you? What message can you decipher from this text?

PRESCRIPTION: SING, DANCE, COOK, PLAY— EXPRESS YOUR INNER SPIRIT

Think about areas in your life where you allow yourself to play and engage your creativity? Perhaps you do not enjoy traditional arts like painting, dance, drawing or singing but instead engage in creative endeavors such as cooking, teaching, problem solving or writing.

- What channels do you use to allow creativity to flow through you and share your talents with others?
- Are there other creative pursuits which you enjoyed in the past and/or would like to engage in more frequently?

Identify any critical voices in your head which might tell you that you are not talented enough to be an artist or share your creativity with others. Write down the judgments and self-criticisms which arise.

Then look back at that critical self-talk and write down rebuttals to each statement. For example, if your inner critic says that you do not have a nice enough voice to sing in your community choir, you may respond, "*Too bad! I am going to allow my inner light and essence to shine anyway! No one other than me can be me and share the gifts and spirit I have within!*"

Get Up and Dance! Think about a song that awakens your spirit and makes you want to sing out loud or dance like no one is watching. Turn on your favorite music, and allow yourself to dance and move freely. Let go. Do not judge yourself or feel pressure to dance the "right" way.

Sing out loud! Allow yourself to be free and not worry about what others might think or how you look or sound. Just feel the music, and allow it to move you in a way that feels great for you. Express the emotions that the music stirs up in your soul with your movements and voice.

Afterwards, sit quietly and reflect on how it felt to express your inner spirit. What was it like to freely let go? How did it feel in your body, mind and spirit to let your soul play and express itself?

CHAPTER 2: Thrive in Loving Authenticity

SOMETIMES WE CAN GET CAUGHT up in life and our efforts to be nice, socially acceptable, cooperative, likeable and "perfect." As you strive to become someone you think others want to see, you can lose sight of who you really are. As you suppress your true desires and hide your inner light, your passion and zest for life may slip away. It is in this place that you need to slow down, take a deep breath and begin to remember what your life is truly about. You need to reconnect with your core purpose, authentic spirit and enthusiasm for living a life aligned with your values, passions and priorities.

Self-observation can occur through many practices. When you are mindful of your interactions, experiences and relationships, you can use these everyday occurrences to further understand and step into your authentic self. We learn about ourselves through our relationships, conversations and daily interactions. If we create the space to mindfully observe ourselves, we can notice our attitudes, patterns, reactions, habits and inclinations. Once you increase your understanding, you may find that some of your current patterns are not working or serving you well. While it can be difficult to recognize, accept and change your habits and reactions, you owe it to yourself and the world around you to live from a place of authentic truth.

Although it can be tempting to feel compelled to change aspects of yourself because you think it will make you more likeable, more successful or more pleasing to others, this almost always simply results in frustration, overwhelm and disappointment. Striving to be anything other than your authentic self deprives you of your true purpose and leaves you feeling frustrated, empty and confused. So many people search for meaning in empty promises, a pint of ice cream, a relationship or even a pharmaceutical pill, but the truth is that you have everything you need within you. You are not broken despite the challenges you have faced in life. You can reconnect with your inner spirit, revive your soul and start to thrive as you steer your life in the direction of your dreams.

Even if you have been building up these fronts to protect yourself and project a self you thought you should be for many, many years, your true spirit is still within. Your light may be hidden under layers of seriousness, fears, bumps and bruises that life has brought your way, but it is possible to peel back those layers and allow that brilliant inner spirit to shine once again. There is a way to get back to living your true and authentic best life. You and the world deserve to have your brilliance shine!

> *"When we align with who we really are, we thrive in our loving authenticity and are already perfect!"*
> *-Dr. Jennifer Weinberg, MD, MPH, MBE*

Knowing oneself is a lifelong practice. We are born as radiant beings, here on this earth to be the presence of love in the world. Early in our lives, however, many of us had experiences that led us to forget this light. Gradually, we may hide our light and hold back our true feelings and gifts rather than risk disappointment, embarrassment or shame.

We must be aware of our thoughts, actions and core desires and step back to observe our reactivity, fears and doubts. It is important

THE WHOLE CURE • 19

to take responsibility for our actions and to embrace our deepest dreams. Learning to observe yourself and reflect on your purpose without judgment and criticism can take practice. But when you watch yourself with objectivity and love, you can reach a deeper level of introspection that allows you to slow down, quiet your mind and look within.

When you view life through a limited frame of reference and adopt a view of the self which you think you *should* be, you can feel small, separate, isolated and defined by your roles in life. But when you stop identifying yourself by others' values or as someone else's daughter, son, father, mother, wife, husband, friend, employee, etc., you can start reconnecting with your authentic self in a truer light. Developing a knowing and connection to your soul, passion and core values enables you to have renewed energy, creativity and freedom.

Your true self is unlimited in nature. It radiates your purpose and a light into the world. When you are living in alignment with this truth, life flows more easily. If you can step back and create a stillness amongst chaos, you can find that place of luminous light and truth within you. You can shift your limited perception of self and liberate greater energy to flow. You cultivate enhanced awareness, purpose and intuition and express more genuine meaning in your thoughts, words and actions. Life becomes less of a struggle, and suffering is relieved. The more you are aware of and living from your true nature, the greater clarity and perspective you cultivate. From this place of true purpose, you move through life with greater joy, ease and ability to effect positive change in yourself and the world around you.

"You are so busy being YOU that you have no idea how utterly unprecedented you are."
-John Green

You have the power to design your life, fill it with your authentic spirit and dare to live it! Instead of feeling stuck in a pattern of unease, unfulfillment and uncertainty where life feels like it is just happening to you, you can take back the reigns. When you have the courage to quiet your mind and step back from your busy life, endless to-do list and constant barrage of demands on your energy and time, you can begin to glimpse the path forward.

Once you recognize this power of your authentic spirit, allow it to flow into the world. Communicating your presence and expressing your gifts allows you to fulfill your core purpose. When you do this, you radiate your unique manifestation and shine forth with authenticity, radiance and grace.

PRESCRIPTION: BREAK YOUR LIMITATIONS AND EMBRACE WONDER

To appreciate with the truth that anything is possible and allow your authentic spirit to shine, you need to reconnect with your core purpose and embrace the infinite possibilities of your life. In order to allow yourself to revive the wonder, curiosity and imagination you were born with, it is necessary to break free of ways of thinking that limit your possibilities and keep you stuck. So often, we become trapped by self-criticism and judgment which holds us back from our full potential.

Reflect on your life and the way you are living. Write down some ways that you are holding back your true spirit and shrouding your inner light.

- In which areas of your life do you feel trapped by limitations of your current thinking?

Think about a time when you allowed your imagination to dream of infinite possibilities.

- How do you see yourself when you embrace the unlimited dimensions of your being?
- Describe what it would be like to live with an unfettered spirit? Place yourself in the stance of an innocent child with an inspired imagination. What do you dream of doing? Who do you dream of being? How can you embrace this wonder-filled experience and the freedom that goes along with it?

From this place of possibility and wonder, look back at the limitations you identified. From this expanded perspective of infinite possibility, write down rebuttals to those areas where you felt stuck. Allow your inner wisdom to teach you creative solutions and opportunities for overcoming these limitations.

- How does it feel to embrace the possibility of living free of these past limitations?
- What would your life be like if you lived from this place of wonder and embraced your creative spirit and imagination?
- What aspect of your unlimited potential would be able to shine forth if you broke down these limiting barriers to shining forth your true light?

Reawaken your truth. Feel what it is like to be truly alive!

PRESCRIPTION: GO WITH THE FLOW

When you are living in alignment with your core truth and radiating your inner light unto the world, life flows with ease. You feel more fully alive. When you find your flow, you experience more natural satisfaction, love and fulfillment each day.

Take some deep breaths to center yourself, and sit quietly. When you really listen deep within, what is the secret inside your heart that speaks of your true purpose? What are you most afraid of? What would you do if you were not afraid? What would you do if you knew you had only one day left on this earth? How do these things relate to your true and authentic calling?

Reflect on ways you are currently living from your authentic truth. What have been the most meaningful times for you in the past few years? What has seemed truly significant in your life in the past month? Identify some experiences you have had in the recent past where you learned something about yourself that felt authentic and true. What did you learn about yourself that you had not recognized before?

How do you allow your inner light to shine into the world? Write down five aspects of your life where you feel a natural flow and ease. Think about the times you feel truly fulfilled. What everyday activities seem to flow seamlessly and with fluidity? These are areas where you are in alignment with your core values and inner truth.

PRESCRIPTION: RADIATE YOUR LIGHT

"Don't you know yet? It is your light that lights the world."
-Rumi

Find a quiet place where you can comfortably rest and will not be disturbed. Lie down or sit comfortably. Close your eyes, and breathe calmly and deeply.

Feel yourself surrounded by healing, glowing energy. Soak in this radiant light, and allow light to emanate from within you to join the endless flow of energy which surrounds you. Feel the pure loving energy all around you and within you. Feel your connection with this glowing light. You and this sea of light are one. Allow yourself to rest in this healing energy. Breathe in light, and radiate out light from your heart. Allow yourself to be nourished by the healing energy all around you and to radiate out love.

When you feel overwhelmed, afraid, stressed or angry, pause and remember this loving energy. Allow this light to flow into your feet and wash over you. Feel this glowing light filling you up and radiating from you heart. As you breathe calmly and deeply in and out, this light is flowing into you and traveling throughout your body. Simultaneously, it radiates out from you back into the world. There is an unlimited, self-renewing current of positive energy in and around you.

Remember that you are filled with luminosity, light and love. Permit this energy to fill you, energize you and strengthen you. Allow this energy to quiet the critical voices in your head and bring you a sense of calm, peace and centeredness. Feel the wisdom that comes with this connection to your inner light. Flow with the ease of acting from your place of divine knowing and glowing spirit.

CHAPTER 3: Beyond Boundaries of Limited Thinking and Perfectionism

WE CAN STRUGGLE WITH acceptance of our true inner light. Many times people compare themselves to others, measure themselves by their pasts and focus on their failures. This can lead to a mindset where you choose experiences based on a false belief of what you think you deserve and attract the wrong people and energy into your life. When you suffer from internal rejection and an inability to feel like who you are and what you have to offer are good enough, life can feel overwhelming and unsatisfying.

Compounding this dissatisfaction can be a compulsion to please others. Do you have a hard time saying no despite feeling resentful after agreeing to do something you really did not want to do? Often we may fail to establish boundaries in our lives, allowing ourselves to be taken advantage of, influenced and distracted from our core values. It is natural to want to be liked and accepted. We do not want to ruffle any feathers or cause any problems. We all want to make others happy, give of ourselves and contribute to our communities, but it is important to know how to set boundaries and align with our priorities as we serve others.

Your ability to establish appropriate boundaries depends on your relationship with yourself and your own core values. Knowing and believing in who you are, what you value and what you are comfortable with allows you to establish and remain loyal to what matters most to you. Being able to set limits or say no to activities, interactions and work that depletes or harms you physically, emotionally or spiritually shows self-love and compassion.

When you have strong, established boundaries which are aligned with your core values you are displaying respect for yourself. Appropriate boundaries allow you to honor your needs and avoid being distracted, consumed and depleted by others' needs. Mature boundaries are about honoring you, your values and your needs and not about judging other people's choices or ideals. When you set appropriate boundaries, you are saying yes to your authentic self. Setting firm and appropriate boundaries is one way to nurture yourself.

Learning to say no does not make you selfish. In fact when you say no to that which is not in alignment with your true purpose and passions, you are saying yes to your inner guide and light. Making time to stand up for your desires and strive toward your own dreams is possible when you are clear about your true priorities and what is most important to you. As you stand true in what you believe in, what you need for yourself and what is a priority for you, you are creating your authentic life!

As a struggling perfectionist, I know what it is like to never feel good enough. For as long as I can remember, I constantly strove to be someone who was praised and respected. I wanted to attain the ultimate level of achievement, and anything less left me feeling empty, discouraged and disappointed with myself. I never felt good enough. This drive to please and be "perfect" arises when we fail to recognize our true light. I struggled to feel accomplished and good enough and was so afraid of judgment from others because I was constantly judging myself.

Too often we live from a place of *should*. We get caught up in living according to how we believe others want us to show up, how we believe we are *supposed* to think, what we think we *ought* to say, how we are trained to believe we *should* or *should not* act. Living in accordance with *shoulds* scatters your energy and fails to fulfill the call of your soul. When you act how you have been conditioned to believe you *should* act according to outside influences, you can lose the connection with your deep inner knowing and shroud your inner light.

This does not have to be your destiny. To live my true purpose, I had to let go of the idea of who I thought I was supposed to be. I needed to discard the idea of who I thought I *should* want to be and reconnect with and accept who I really was. As I learned to accept that I was more than good enough, I became truly free. I could shine and live my life aligned with my purpose and true passions.

You are not the result of your past, the product of your environment, the outcome of your conditioning nor the consequences of your experiences. You are not the story which others tell about you. You are good enough and so much more. Learning to break free of these limiting stories and the fear of unworthiness allows you to live a richer life that is more aligned with your authenticity. Embrace the inner radiance that allows you to move into your greatness.

When you are aligned with this true spirit and inner guidance, security, contentment and peace come effortlessly, and life flows more easily. You can follow your instincts, trust your true calling and recognize your intuition. You will find indisputable inspiration within you. Our thoughts, our emotions and even our physical bodies are constantly evolving, allowing us to shift our stories. This opens up an energy of possibility where immense shifts can occur.

The first step to finding this peace is accepting yourself for who you really are. Acknowledge that you can be who you want to and are meant to be and not what you think others want to see. Know that you are already enough and do not need outside approval to tell you that this is true. These can be difficult lessons to learn, but once you accept yourself and your truth, you will be free to live the life you have imagined. When you are able to accept and love your true self, you open up the possibility of attracting all that you desire. As you break down the walls of limited thinking that previously kept your hopes and dreams out of reach, you invite abundance and boundless potential to flow in.

"You alone are enough. You have nothing to prove to anyone."
-Maya Angelou

Embracing your truth and allowing your inner light to shine is a process. It can bring immense freedom and ease into your life. Awakening to your immeasurable potential begins with seeing and acknowledging your truth. Awareness can be an effective tool to help shift your mindset from fear and unease to love and peace, from criticism to compassion and from conditional to unconditional love.

As you open your awareness to your true desires and potential, you can begin to accept and live from a place of authenticity. You can see your inner critic and perfectionist. You can acknowledge the judgment, fears, criticisms and stories clouding your vision. Through this recognition, you can bring light into the darkness and consciousness to the unconscious patterns. This creates a powerful shift in perception. As you cultivate this internal awareness, you build self-approval and satisfaction and connect more intimately with your true inner light.

Becoming more aware of your heart's true whisperings allows you to start to share that which is in your heart with others. As you share from your heart without fear of criticism, feedback or judgment, you show up as the best version of yourself. You stop hiding the parts of yourself that you assumed others would not approve of nor accept. You begin to give fully, speak openly, share your true passions and be more vulnerable.

This opens you up, regardless of outcome, and invites space for joy and authentic satisfaction to fill your life. Being able to share yourself, your heart and your being with the world from a place of authenticity and vulnerability is so powerful! Your true job is to generously and unconditionally share your inner light and surrender the rest. This will bring you greater peace, power and satisfaction. Everything will begin to flow more abundantly and naturally.

You can consciously choose to let go of old stories, ideas that you have formed about what you should be or how you should act, the boxes you have trapped yourself in and the need to prove something to others. Old stories and untrue beliefs can become quite engrained in our thinking, yet this conditioning keeps us stuck in situations, patterns and circumstances that hold us back. Instead you can choose to embrace your loving light and accept the amazing being your find within!

When you release misleading beliefs and fully embrace who you are without criticism, resistance and judgment, you liberate the full potential and true loving presence that is your authentic soul. As you surrender your limiting mindset and unleash your brilliance, you begin to live your authentic life in harmony with your true self!

PRESCRIPTION: PASSIONATE PRIORITIES

A priority is something that is aligned with your ultimate life purpose and calling. It is that thing that is so important to you that it has to be done, even if this requires saying no to other commitments and requests. To live a life of passion, purpose and authenticity, it is vital to make your hopes, dreams and true desires priorities.

Take time to reflect on your true passions, hopes, dreams and desires for your life. Write down a list of your current priorities and how they will move you closer towards your purpose, hopes and authentic life.

Then look at your calendar and schedule in tasks that align with these priorities. Schedule all the steps you need to take in order to feel whole and committed to you. As you schedule these tasks you are making a commitment to you and your passionate purpose. Scheduling these tasks into your calendar makes them real.

Once you have blocked out these prioritized actions, the leftover time is available for you to make outside commitments that align with your purpose. Beyond that, you have a clear indication to say no to anything which does not fit into those priorities. Give yourself permission to say yes to your dreams and desires, and get comfortable saying no to the rest.

This is how you will best serve your community as well. As you care for yourself and create the space to nurture your needs, you become a better community member, family member, coworker, partner and caregiver. When you are living a life that you truly desire and believe in, you are putting your best self out into the world.

Allow yourself the time and space to let your dreams manifest. You will find that this gives you a sense of freedom and alignment. Saying no is vital to success and authenticity. As you practice living this way, you will find that internal conflict and resentment melts away. Celebrate stepping into your authenticity and putting yourself first!

PRESCRIPTION: SHINE YOUR OWN LIGHT

We are born as radiant beings here to be the presence of love in the world. Early in our lives, however, many of us had experiences that led us to forget or shroud this light. Little by little, we may hide our true feelings and gifts rather than risk disapproval, failure, or shame.

How will you choose to shine this week?

Use the following affirmation to remind you of your mission to serve your authentic purpose and the world with your inner light. Place it several places you will see it often during the week, such as on the refrigerator, on your car dashboard, on your bathroom mirror and by the kitchen sink.

Affirmation: "I am totally independent of the good or bad opinion of others!"

Each time you see this statement, read it silently or out loud to yourself. Feel the words resonating throughout your being.

What would it feel like if this affirmation was totally true for you? How would your life change? Contemplate your desired reality as you engage in this prescription.

PRESCRIPTION: CREATE A CORE VALUE MAP

It is important to be clear on what you value the most, how you choose to live your life, who you truly are and what ideals you uphold. Find a space and time where you can be without distraction. Sit comfortably and quiet your mind. Take a few deep breaths in through your nose and out through your mouth. Relax and get centered.

Reflect and journal about your core values:

- Who are you? Focus on your core values, desires, dreams and passions instead of defining yourself by your roles, profession or relationships.
- What are your passions?
- What do you value?
- What ideals do you strive to uphold?
- What are you comfortable with? What is outside of your comfort zone?
- What matters most to you in life?

Once you have freely reflected on these ideas, it is time to create a core value map. Gather images, words, quotes, materials and anything else that reflects your core values for you. Create a collage, image, song, photograph or other expression that establishes what your core values mean for you. Place this symbol of your true values in a place you will see it often.

PRESCRIPTION: BRAINSTORM BOUNDARIES

It is important to be clear about your needs and boundaries. You need to be able to communicate your boundaries decisively, both verbally and through your actions and behaviors. If you say you will not tolerate an action but then give in here and there, people will test, push and disrespect your limits. This can create confusion and chaos in your relationships.

Life is complicated and you will find yourself in situations where your boundaries are challenged. It can be helpful to decide ahead of time what the consequences will be when someone pushes your boundaries.

When your boundaries arise out of your core values and you are clear with yourself and others about what you need, believe in and respect, you will remain steadfast in your commitment to respect your boundaries. When you have clear, strong boundaries, you will not get upset or emotional when others try to test them. For example, if monogamy is one of your core values and you have decided that you will not accept a relationship where this is not valued, you will leave the relationship when your husband cheats on you.

Find a space and time where you can be without distraction. Sit comfortably and quiet your mind. Take a few deep breaths in through your nose and out through your mouth. Relax and get centered.

Remember that boundaries are about honoring you, your values and your needs and not about judging others. Reflect and journal about some key boundaries that reflect your core values and the corresponding consequences which you find appropriate to apply when someone crosses them.

Remain authentic to yourself by demonstrating consistency in your words and action. Say what you need and act accordingly. As you become clearer with yourself about your true values and resulting boundaries, you will be more assured in your communication.

CHAPTER 4: Intentional Action Guided by Inner Wisdom

DO YOU TRUST YOUR INTUITION? Often we hear that little inner voice that is striving to direct us, but we may second guess it or suppress it. We look outward for guidance or start to rely on other people's opinions or ideas instead of our inner truth.

The mind can be a busy place. We are often consumed with thoughts, anxieties, judgments and perceptions. As these thoughts flood our minds, we rarely notice where they actually come from or how they impact us. But if we can quiet our minds and find a stillness amidst our busy lives, we can separate ourselves from our thoughts and reconnect with our intuition.

"Intuition is a sense of knowing how to act spontaneously without needing to know why."
-Sylvia Clare

Heart-Centered Decisions

We all have goals and dreams. Yet it can be easy to get caught up in the small distractions around us. Our minds can become overwhelmed with worrying about what others are doing, how we think we should live or who we assume we should be. In the midst of chasing our dreams, the mind has a tendency to get caught up in fears, doubts and thoughts. These anxieties can drown out your intuition and cause you to drift away from the present.

It is often easier to trust your intuition when it involves little things, but big decisions can seem overwhelming. Facing decisions that impact your life in substantial ways can trigger apprehension, hesitation, self-criticism and indecision. This can throw you into a cycle of inaction, second-guessing and stagnation that holds you back or throws you off course from your authentic, passion-driven path.

When we drift away from the present moment, what we see tends to be misconstrued and confused by the chatter of our thoughts, worries and emotions. This skewed perception of the world can lead us to create stories to which we may become attached. We may internalize the outside world and become attached to memories of our past and speculations of our future. When you latch onto a story and give it an excessive amount of energy, you create obsessions and delusions. These pull you out of the present moment and drown out your intuition.

To truly see, you need to look more deeply. You need to release your preconceived patterns and remain open to seeing with wisdom and intuition. You need to trust yourself and the universe. To access this inner knowing, you need to let go and surrender to the stillness of the present moment. When you are able to detach from the identification with your thoughts, you are able to grow in the now. As you cultivate awareness and mindfulness, you will grow in your ability to recognize true wisdom and be able to separate speculation from intuition.

The truth is, your purpose-driven self can only exist in the present moment. You need to be able to remain in the here and now in order to move forward. You can only be in touch with your inner wisdom and intuition when you are able to separate yourself from the chatter of your thoughts. In the present, your authentic self can shine.

As you slow down and listen, your intuition will become more distinct. You will more easily recognize that drive that comes from your inner knowing. You will notice an ease and flow when making decisions. When you listen to your intuition and take action in accordance with it, you will feel a gentle flow. Life will have a natural impulse, and amazing things will happen.

"Truth is by nature self-evident. As soon as you remove the cobwebs of ignorance that surround it, it shines clear."
-Mahatma Gandhi

Inner Wisdom

Fortunately, your intuition is always there to guide you in the right direction. You can master the ability to tap into your intuition easily and naturally, every time. A key step in allowing your inner wisdom to guide your actions is learning to listen. You need to remain fully present, open and receptive to receive exactly what you need to know and understand. When your heart speaks, pay careful attention.

One way to become more adept at truly listening to the wisdom within and around you is to practice meditation and allow yourself quiet stillness each day. As you find this calm space, you can connect with your intuition more naturally. Over time, you will develop more trust in your inner guidance in every moment.

It is also important to become clear about how your intuition shows up. Your inner wisdom may be that clear, firm voice in your head or a more subtle whisper from your heart. Intuition can manifest in many forms, involving auditory, visual, kinesthetic and subtle energy. This inner knowing engages multisensory perception. It may show up as a specific physical sensation or a subtle knowing.

"When your heart speaks, pay careful attention. Listen."
-Dr. Jennifer Weinberg, MD, MPH, MBE

Your sophisticated inner guidance system allows you to interpret the world in a way that goes beyond that which you can perceive with your five senses. When you utilize your senses, you pay attention to that which is outside of you. Yet when you embrace your intuition, you are able to pay attention to what is happening within you as well. As you pay attention to how your inner wisdom shows up, you will learn to instantly recognize it.

In this enlightened state, you become more adept at tapping into imagination, creativity, unused talents and instincts. True wisdom is listening to and purposefully acting on your inner knowledge. When that inner wisdom arises, trust it and take action. The more you listen to and act on the guidance you receive, the easier it will be to hear that inner voice in the future. As you practice placing trust in your intuition, the fear, doubt and ego that can sidetrack you will be less likely to get in the way.

Give yourself permission to trust your inner guidance system. Allow yourself the stillness to listen. And cultivate the courage to act upon the decisions towards which you are guided. As your trust in your intuition grows, your knowledge of your true self develops. As you align with your inherent intuition, you are lead to your truth, your purpose and your path. When you do this, you will be amazed at the flow of your life and what you can accomplish. Connecting with and listening to your intuition will lead you to a more fulfilling life!

PRESCRIPTION: ACTUATING WISDOM

In order to recognize and act upon your inner guidance system, it is necessary to learn to consistently listen to your intuition. Find a quiet place where you will not be disturbed, and take some time to reflect on and journal about the following concepts.

To begin activating your connection with your inner wisdom, think about a time when you were struggling with a decision or striving to understand a situation, and you found the answer within. Remember a time when you faced a dilemma and made a decision based on a sense of inner knowing.

- What was it like to follow a path which felt right to you even if it was not the straightforward, seemingly logical choice at the time or if you did not blindly follow the normal rules?

Describe what it was like to realize that the answers were within you. Write in detail about the way you felt when you connected with your inner wisdom and intuition. What was it like for you to experience that inner sense of knowing what to do? Evoke the details of how it felt to access and trust this awareness.

Describe how you experience decisions. Do you struggle with confusion, desperation, frustration, doubt and/or uncertainty? Or are you able to recognize the simple awareness and knowing of your inner intelligence?

- How do you typically tap into your intuition?
- What is it like for you to listen and tap into your inner knowing?
- What makes it hard to listen to and trust your inner guidance?

Reflect on how you can learn from your past experiences with accessing your inner wisdom. Remember what it is like to recognize your intuition on a mental, physical and emotional level. Use this deepened awareness to recognize and honor your inner wisdom as you allow it to guide you through life!

PRESCRIPTION: SLEEP ON IT

Our brains take in many things we encounter during the day which we may not consciously recognize. These concepts are stored in the brain and can emerge during the REM stage of sleep when the brain connects ideas in new and creative ways. During this time of sleep, the brain solves problems and brings wisdom to decisions that we are struggling with in our waking lives.

The brain taps into images it has stored, ideas you have processed and intuitive knowing to put the pieces together and try out new alternatives and solutions. During sleep, the brain may gain awareness that can lead to practical insights that you can apply in your waking life. Dreams can allow you to move past blocks and see solutions that are not apparent to your logical, conscious mind.

Think of a decision with which you are struggling or a challenging circumstance in your life. Before going to sleep, write down a problem and your thoughts about the situation. Set it aside and go to sleep. Allow your intuition to process the issue as you sleep. Keep your journal by your bed. As you awaken, allow the mind to cultivate awareness of solutions that were previously shrouded.

Use that time first thing in the morning when you are just awakening and not quite fully conscious to tap into your unconscious mind and uncover the inner work that was done while you were sleeping. Listen to what arises from your inner guidance system, and allow it to lead you on your path of transformation.

Allow a stream of consciousness to flow first thing in the morning. Write down whatever arises. Begin by writing down anything you remember from your dreams. Think about all that the things you are grateful for in your life, from the simple to the profound. Write down whatever comes into your mind and flows onto the paper, without censoring, judging or doubting. Trust that whatever arises is exactly what you need to hear and know in that moment.

Reflect on the following questions with your identified challenges and dilemmas in mind.

- What would peace do in this situation?
- What would calm do in this situation?
- What would fearless knowing do in this situation?

As you practice this over time, you will send a message to the inner workings of your brain that you are prepared to listen and accept your inner guidance. As you are open and present to hearing that which is within, more and more insight will be revealed. You can express the repressed thoughts and emotions you are stuffing inside and hear the messages within.

This process will allow you to develop a deeper more direct relationship with your inner self and be able to more clearly perceive your intuition. Allow your intuition to show you the solutions.

PRESCRIPTION: RECOGNIZE YOUR INNER GUIDANCE SYSTEM

We can experience intuition in a variety of ways. Your inner guidance may come to you through your sensory experiences, through dreams or as a feeling of knowing. Intuition is grounded in what we feel rather than in what we think. It can be easiest to recognize your intuition in the quiet moments when you are able to step away from the chatter of the mind and logical thinking process. Activities such as dancing, drumming, yoga, meditation, guided imagery, prayer and spending time in nature can help set the stage for hearing that wise voice within you.

Your inner guidance system is there to help you find your true path when you can learn to recognize and listen to its wisdom. Use this exercise to cultivate your understanding of how your intuition speaks to you.

Find a quiet place where you can sit or lie down comfortably and not be disturbed. Close your eyes, and take a few deep breaths. Begin to focus inward. Notice the flow of the air in through your nose as you breathe in. Feel your chest and belly rise and fall with each inhale and exhale. Notice any sensations, tingling or thoughts that arise.

Begin to bring your attention to an image of something that you love to do. Imagine yourself in a situation that brings you pleasure and true joy. Feel in your body the reaction you have when you think about this experience. What are you feeling? Where in your body do you notice this sense of contentment? Then let go of that situation.

Now think about something that you know is not in alignment with who you are or something you know is bad for you. Feel what it is like in your body when you are imagining this situation. What types of sensations arise in your body when you imagine yourself engaging in this experience? Where do you feel these in your body? Then let go of that situation.

Notice the difference between the expansion and excitement you experience when you embrace an experience that resonates with your core self versus the contracted, unsettled sensation in your body that arises when considering an unpleasant or misaligned situation.

This is one way you can begin to distinguish your guiding inner wisdom from fear, doubt and resistance to moving forward. When you are considering a significant decision or life circumstance, pause and ask yourself how it feels in your body. Does it create expansion and excitement or contraction and chaotic energy?

When your intuition speaks, you will generally notice a sense of opening and a potential for growth and forward movement. There are many signals that can indicate that your intuition is speaking to you. You may feel goose bumps, a sense of relaxation or a leaning into a situation when your intuition is guiding you towards something that is aligned with your purpose. You may have some nervous excitement or trepidation over the prospect of acting on your dreams, but this resistance is coming from the mind and not the core intuitive self.

On the other hand, when your intuition is guiding you away from something that is not in alignment with what is best for you, you will feel a contraction or a blocked or stuck sensation in your body. This may arise as a tightening or sinking feeling, a lump or constriction, a crawling sensation on your skin or a sense of being drained. Often these sensations are experienced in the heart, throat or gut.

Conversely, when you are stuck in your thoughts and emotions and being steered by fear instead of intuition, you may feel these sensations coming from your head, neck, face or shoulders. This is usually just your mind becoming anxious with the thought of change, growth and new experiences and is not usually your intuition trying to stop you from an experience that is not right for you.

As you become more aware of how your inner guidance system speaks to you, you can more easily tap into it to help you make decisions. You will begin to more easily ride this energetic wave of guidance and listen to the messages it contains. Learning to become aware of when you are receiving an intuitive message can help your guidance system to become stronger.

PRESCRIPTION: STEP INTO YOUR POWER

Find a place where you will not be interrupted. Sit comfortably and close your eyes. Bring your attention inward. Take a few deep breaths. Relax any areas where you are holding tension.

Bring a vision of yourself to mind. See yourself on a path with a bright spotlight glowing ahead. Walk towards that place of light. Imagine yourself stepping into your place of power. You are in the spotlight, basking in this glowing, empowering, loving light. You are the creator of your life and path. Everything you have experienced and done in your life up until this point has prepared you for this moment. All that you have withstood and celebrated has led you to this moment. You are strong and proud of all that you have accomplished. You uphold your values and live from your authentic truth. Your soul is vibrant, and your intuition is strong. Soak in this light and all that it brings and celebrates. Revel in these positive feelings. Feel the positive energy and vibrations filling you in the here and now.

You are your future now and moving forward. Look forward and create your path. Allow your intuition to guide its shape and flow. Your destiny is unfolding as you allow your intuition to guide you. You have embraced your passionate purpose. Your internal guidance system has all the answers and maps out the route for you to follow. All you need to do is remain open and present to see the signs along the way. As you step onto this evolving path into your future you are arriving at your authentic purpose, in just the time and place where you belong.

CHAPTER 5: A Clear Vision for Intentional Goals

PART OF RECONNECTING with a life you love involves choosing an existence that aligns with your vision and desires. This involves clarifying your dreams, setting defined intentions and crafting a lifestyle that aligns with your desires on a daily basis. As you become more engaged in practices that shape your present and build into your future, you bring to life a larger and more intentional purpose.

Vision

When you are in touch with your intuition, core values, desired outcomes, inspirations and aspirations, you send a clear message about what you wish to accomplish and embody. Vision involves having the clarity to act in alignment with that which you envision creating. Having a clear vision for your life and putting it out there allows you to visualize, dream and manifest what you desire for your future self.

Elucidating your vision involves taking time to find the stillness of the present moment. As you step back from the chaos of your regular routine, you can take a more distinct look at the larger picture of your journey and what you are moving towards. It is important to take time to slow down, pause and listen so that you can reflect deeply on what you have learned thus far on your journey through life and how you can apply those lessons towards your next steps.

As you gather your inner wisdom, insight arises, and you take well-shepherded steps forward toward an improved future. The first step towards reaching your intentional goals is to develop the ability to envision a flourishing future in which you easily align with your passionate purpose. Acting from your authentic nature ignites your vision and fuels your commitment to achieving a more purposeful life.

As you become clear about what you need and focus on your core desired objectives, you can identify that bigger dream that will bring you satisfaction and motivation for the long-term. Instead of darting from one superficial desire to another and only attaining momentary happiness, you are able to overcome overwhelm and achieve those big life goals without feeling restricted, overworked or exhausted.

When you allow your energy to focus on your highest potential and give your mind space to reach into your genuine desires, you begin to form a more complete and accurate sense of what you are truly seeking. Your goals and desires become clearer, and your true aspirations and core purpose are revealed. You uncover and more fully comprehend that which you are truly seeking.

Becoming clear about that which brings you enduring internal gratification leads you towards a vision that will transform your dreams into a meaningful path. Your clear vision has no limitations and moves you towards your intentional aspirations.

Your vision includes many aspects of who you are and how you live your life. It encompasses the gifts and passions you have, your goals and dreams and that which awakens your heart and soul. Together these attributes combine to create a drive and desire which propels your life forward.

"To accomplish great things, we must not only act, but also dream, not only plan, but also believe."
- Anatole France

A vision for your physical, emotional, mental and spiritual wellness can take many forms. It can encompass a written declaration of your desired outcomes, behaviors and values or a visual representation of your dreams in the form of a collage, poem or other form of creative expression.

Bringing your desires to life and giving them vitality helps you understand your true goals, dreams and longings. When you connect with and listen to your intuition, you can create a clear and concrete pathway for constructing your vision and reaching your goals. It is possible to translate your ultimate dreams and grand vision for your life into actionable goals to create the life you want on your terms. A clear vision, inspired intention and corresponding goals are important, but taking action to execute them allows the true magic to happen!

Intentional Goals

To find true meaning and fulfillment in your life experience, it is important to recognize your passions and acknowledge your full potential. When you live with purpose and meaning, you will make decisions that support your intentions. Establishing your intentions allows you to commit to actions which align with your inner values in order to manifest the greater vision for your life.

Becoming clear about what matters most to you, leads you to make better choices and find more satisfaction in life. This makes you feel pleased about yourself as you fulfill your core vision and accomplish your true purpose. If you set your intention to live in a healthy and meaningful way, you will take actions that support this intention. Your heart-centered intentions will encourage your personal evolution while simultaneously contributing to the larger whole as well.

Although at times our busy lives and the chaos of our minds may seem to get in the way of our dreams, when we disconnect from the chatter and settle into our grounded purpose, we gain the power to manifest our dreams and achieve our deepest goals. You have the power to set your intentions and open to your divine purpose. When you are aligned and connected with your soul-centered intentions, you will receive as much peace, love and joy as you believe you deserve.

Your big visions, dreams and goals are related more to who you are at your authentic core than to what you do or the roles you carry out in your life. Becoming clear about how you want to feel and the energy you wish to project into the world allows you to design your goals in sync with your authentic self.

Your actions and intentions will embody your values and allow you to grow, evolve and flourish as you move towards your goals. Framing your intentional goals in this way bestows innate value to the process of moving towards your goals. In this way, the awakening and expression of your larger vision and the small steps you take each day to uphold your intentions hold innate value. These standards become independent of results and provide meaning beyond simply leading to the attainment or failure of your goal. When your goals are grounded more in your being rather than doing, your life has greater freedom and ease.

To begin to recognize and clarify your heart-centered goals that truly reflect your inner light, you need to start discovering those things that have been holding you back from living in alignment with your authentic purpose. Often emotions like fear and doubt, feelings of overwhelm and outside pressures and influences distract us from achieving our goals and dreams. These emotions tend to keep us stuck and limit our potential.

Often it is the things that scare us the most that we need to do, try, think or say in order to have true growth. Fear may manifest in your life as negativity, self-doubt, judgment, criticism, anxiety, hopelessness, panic or worry. These emotions and the resulting thoughts tend to hold you back from reaching for your goals and living your true passionate purpose. Through the prescriptions in this chapter, you will begin to recognize these fear-based emotions and work towards moving beyond them towards your authentic, vibrant life!

To cultivate your dreams and reach your big, juicy goals, you need to identify your deepest desires. When you are clear on your intentions for how you want to live your life, you can reframe your thoughts to view the world around you as supportive to the achievement of those goals. Focusing your attention on what you want and deserve and being fully aware and present in your daily life accelerates the achievement of your goals and the manifestation of your dreams. Take the time to dream, and envision yourself enjoying this new reality you are building. In each moment, choose your thoughts, words and actions with intention. You create your reality!

PRESCRIPTION: UNWRAP YOUR GIFTS

You were born with unique and powerful talents and gifts. Your skills, abilities, passions and talents make you who you are and give you the power to reach your goals and create an authentic passionate life. You may recognize some of these gifts and employ them in your daily life, while others may remain unwrapped and unused.

You may have been gifted talents including creativity, adaptability, resourcefulness, athleticism, grace, a positive attitude, kindness, a beautiful voice, the ability to teach, or the facility to eloquently express inspired thoughts. Think about your unique talents, gifts and abilities with regards to the following questions.

- What gifts are you currently using in your life? How do you employ these talents, skills and abilities to reach your goals and create a purposeful life? What do these passions allow you to achieve and give to others?
- Which gifts have you not yet unwrapped? What talents and skills are sitting idle in your life? Do you have passions and abilities that could help you achieve your goals which you are not currently using?

- What steps do you need to take to be able to fully employ these unopened gifts?
- What will happen when you engage and utilize these skills and talents? How will unwrapping all of your talents and allowing them to impact the world change your reality and contribute to your vision of your most authentic life?

With the enhanced clarity you have received from exploring and unwrapping your gifts, you can more clearly step into your power and recognize your passionate purpose. Think about who you truly are and what your full vision is for your life. Complete the following statement:

I am _____ *who has many gifts such as*

_____, _____ *and*

_____. *I love to* _____.

I choose to unwrap my gifts of _____

_____, *and* _____

and use them to _____.

PRESCRIPTION: EMBRACING A SOUL VISION

Becoming clear on your desired vision for your life and what you wish to accomplish allows you to visualize, dream and actualize what you desire for your future self. You can conceptualize your vision in the form of a written letter, a visual collage, a poem or another form of creative expression.

Think of your vision as a declaration of your core values, authentic behaviors, inspirations, desires and aspirations. Consider the greatest potential of your future self. Embrace a complete sense of what you truly seek to create in and with your life.

THE WHOLE CURE • 46

In your soul vision statement or expression, include a description of how your authentic self exists in body, mind and spirit. Think about the ways in which you carry out your purpose and use your gifts.

- How do you express yourself?
- How do you embrace your passionate purpose?
- What values do you uphold?
- What is your vision for your physical self and health?
- What are your daily activities and how do they align with and reflect your core values?

Describe your motivations, inspirations and aspirations.

- How do you approach challenges?
- Where do you seek guidance and support?
- What reminds you of and reignites your true passions?

Fully embrace and depict your vision for your authentic passionate life. Use your imagination and means of expression to bring your deepest dreams and desires to life. Energize your vision, and allow it to illuminate a clear path towards crafting appropriate goals and taking concrete steps to fulfill your vision.

Use your drawings, writings, pictures and collages to capture and concentrate on your success. Mentally see yourself living your soul vision. Examine how you will react, communicate, convey your desires and articulate your needs. Visualize yourself handling decisions and challenges with grace, decisiveness, self-assurance and a calm, confident and centered attitude.

Experience what it will feel like to actualize your vision with all of your senses. What will it smell, feel, taste, sound and look like? Fully embrace the reality of this victory!

PRESCRIPTION: PAUSE, REFLECT AND SET YOUR INTENTIONS

Establishing your goals and intentions involves getting clear on your overarching vision and envisioning a future outcome. Once you have connected with your vision for where you are going, you can take steps to plan, apply dedication and work towards living a life that allows you to achieve that future.

Your personal goals provide direction for your life and help you organize your energy and time. Goals involve a focus on hopes and dreams for the future. They lead you to envisage what is next. How will you feel when you reach that point?

Think about three challenges you are currently working on.

- How are these situations, relationships and/or struggles hindering you from reaching your highest intentions and goals?
- Make a list of all the activities, people, experiences and dreams that are impacted by your current state of being, whether you are struggling with toxicity, health challenges, lack of energy, overwhelm or brain fog.

Reflect back on three large obstacles which you have overcome in the past year.

- What lessons have you learned through the struggle?
- What have you discovered about yourself in the process?
- What qualities have you strengthened as you tackled these challenges and grew as a result?

Recall three ways in which you have grown in a positive way in the past year.

- How have you moved closer to your authentic self?
- What steps have you taken to manifest your passionate purpose?
- How have the small steps you have taken carried you forward and helped you grow as a person?

Think about the overarching vision you have for your life. Examine the larger picture of where you are now, where you have been, what you have journeyed through and what you are moving towards.

Allow yourself to openly explore your biggest dreams and the vision you have for your authentic life.

Imagine the possibilities, without censorship or outside influences. Your vision has no boundaries. It is that which ignites your passion and fuels your commitment to do whatever it takes to achieve your authentic purpose.

Imagine living in alignment with your larger vision. Allow yourself to embody the sensations, mindset and energy you will experience as you make your vision a reality.

- What emotions, feelings and outcomes do you hope to experience as you carry out your intentions this year?
- How does it feel in your body when you are acting, thinking and experiencing life in accordance with this ideal?

Noticing what it feels like to be living in alignment with your greater vision and intentions, identify three qualities or character traits you want to cultivate as you move forward to help you manifest your vision and goals.

- How will these energies move you towards your intentions?

With your overarching vision in mind, identify three intentional goals for the next year. Committing to and envisioning your goals can help you take key steps to reaching them and creating the life of your dreams!

Now, think about each of these goals and imagine potential obstacles that might arise or stand in the way of achieving your intentions. Develop a solution for each of these challenges.

As you achieve each of your intentional goals, what will you experience? Reflect on and identify the desired outcomes, feelings, emotions and circumstances that you will gain as you realize your intentions. Feel what it is like to have brought your goals to fruition. Visualize and sense what it is like to have achieved these aspirations.

PRESCRIPTION: SCHEDULING SUCCESS ONE STEP AT A TIME

To reach your full potential and live a life of passion and purpose, it is important to set and reach meaningful and obtainable goals. You need to break down each dream you have into achievable and clearly-defined goals that gradually build to your ultimate desires.

When you engage in small but consistent steps which are aligned with your vision and intentions, you will get results. Each day, move toward achieving your goals and use your time wisely, and your entire life will change. Intentional action brings success!

To manifest your vision and reach your goals, it is important to own your passion and core values and believe that you already possess the gifts, abilities and talents you need. Anchor your dreams in reality, and commit to making them come true.

In order to remain focused on your larger dreams and not get sidetracked by the chaos of life, it is important to effectively manage your time. To ensure that the truly important things get accomplished, you can work on focusing on the projects and steps that directly align with your greater vision first. As you do this, you will find that the smaller tasks will naturally fall into place.

Think about your large dreams and intentions and how they fit within your ultimate vision. Your intentions arise from that which matters most to you and help align your actions with your inner values and morals. You are constantly navigating through your life and can strive to live from your intentions as a daily practice.

• What is the overarching vision you have for your life?

Intentions are something you live by each day in the present moment. They guide how you approach your day-to-day life as a mindful, aware and confident being. Intentions shape how you carry out your passionate purpose. Your intentions embody how you aim to be and exist in the world. For example, you can intend to be present, loving, fearless, passionate, awake, vibrant, peaceful and/or happy. When you are aligned with your intentions, your actions take on a quality that allows you to move towards your true goals as your greatest self guides your action.

- Write down three intentions which you hold that arise from your overarching vision.

Based on your overarching vision and intentions, reflect back on the intentional goals you have set for this year. Break down your goals into smaller tasks and steps. Start by scheduling the larger projects into your agenda, allowing realistic amounts of time to work on achieving the steps leading up to your goals. Tackle each piece individually. Make sure you have a concrete, measureable outcome tied to the accomplishment of each task. Strive to find the joy in the process and triumph instead of making it burdensome or punishing.

Multitasking distracts us and dilutes our energy. On the other hand, focused attention leads to sustained productivity. Carefully review your schedule and set yourself up for productive success. Become aware of where you waste your time and energy. Focus on the moment and take it one task and step at a time. It is not about juggling as much as possible or constantly multitasking, which can drain and scatter your energy.

- Think about which items are most important and why?
- What must you do to ensure you accomplish your greatest priorities?
- How can you change habits to better manage your time?

To devote yourself to what truly matters to you, make a concerted effort to cut out distractions like surfing the Internet or constantly checking your email. Allow your mind to focus on the present moment without becoming caught up in fixating on the past or worrying about the future. Enjoy the moments, reminding yourself that you are exactly where you need to be in the here and now.

PRESCRIPTION: MY MANTRA

Cultivating self-awareness and positive self-talk can make a powerful impact on the way you experience your life and reach your intentional goals. Positive affirmations and personal mantras may seem simple, but the effects of consistently using these positive statements can support growth and evolution in your life.

You attract what you focus on, so when you focus on abundance and positivity, that is what you cultivate. Thoughts result in feelings which influence your actions and ultimately lead to results. So in order to realize the goals and results you desire, you need to begin with altering your thought patterns. To change your thoughts so that they empower you instead of limit you, you can begin by recognizing and changing the pattern of your self-talk.

We continuously speak to ourselves, creating a narrative that impacts our feelings, intentions and actions. What we say impacts how we think and feel about ourselves. Unfortunately we are often our own worst critics, and this is very clear in the things we say to ourselves day in and day out.

As you repeatedly criticize yourself, this negative self-talk seeps into your subconscious. Overtime, you may repeat these statements over and over again without even realizing it. If these thoughts become too dominant, they may begin to form your beliefs and dominate your reality.

Positive affirmations can help to break this viscous cycle. These constructive statements serve to neutralize the negative inner critic and over time begin to replace limiting self-talk with loving, empowering thoughts. This allows you to embrace the possibilities and opportunities in your life instead of being held back by what you perceive as obstacles.

Positive affirmations can help to break this viscous cycle of negative self-beliefs. These statements serve to neutralize the negative inner critic. Over time begin to replace your limiting self-talk with loving, empowering thoughts.

You can make your own affirmation cards with positive statements that resonate with you! Place these affirmation cards around your house, work and car where you will see them regularly. Each day, read the affirmations out loud while looking into your reflection in the mirror. Say them with power, conviction and faith.

"What you think, you become.

What you feel, you attract.

What you imagine, you create."
-Buddha

In addition to using positive affirmations, try creating your own mantra. Choose a simple, personalized statement that encapsulates your intentional goal. For example, *'I am an empowered entrepreneur who runs a successful, heart-centered business.'*

Place this mantra around the spaces in which you spend your time. Repeat your mantra throughout the day. Read your affirmation out loud while looking at your reflection in the mirror. Say these statements with power, conviction and faith. Take time to sit quietly and visualize yourself achieving your dreams. As you do this, you are conditioning your mind for success.

While it is not always easy to create an authentic life based on your intuition and passionate purpose, following your heart and owning your path allows great things to happen. Your vision is real. Allow yourself to be guided along your path towards achieving your greatest dreams. You are an inspiration. Believe in yourself, your purpose and your strength!

THE WHOLE CURE • 53

CHAPTER 6: Slow Down to Be Peace in the Ease of the Present Moment

SO MANY OF US GO THROUGH life with a nagging yearning for something more. Our lives move fast. We stay busy running from one commitment to another. In our modern world, we are often disconnected from the natural rhythms of nature. The daily grind makes it difficult to maintain balance. We work long hours, are bombarded with information and take less and less time for rest and relaxation. Busy has become the default state of our lives.

Amidst this hectic pace, thoughts flood our minds, often clouding our wisdom and intuition with the chatter of doubts, judgments and confusion. Society bombards us with messages that we need more material things. Our past experiences scar us with beliefs that we are not good enough, not worthy enough or not accomplished enough. This chaotic frenzy can make it difficult to connect with your authentic self and recognize, listen to and follow your passionate purpose.

THE WHOLE CURE • 54

You may experience a sense of hunger for something more when you fail to consistently find stillness in the present moment. Deep down you may feel a sense of unease, disturbance and disappointment. It may always seem like you are not being or having enough. You may cling, suffer, struggle and doubt your choices and existence. It can feel like life is a bucket with a hole in the bottom. No matter how hard you strive to continuously fill your vessel with meaning and satisfaction, it seems futile. This cycle of struggle, frustration and meaninglessness creates distress and unease.

Frequently, we attend to this void by acquiring more and more material things, achieving another title or degree or indulging in a sweet treat or glass of wine. Or we may hold our breath, waiting for "something" to happen to or for us. Although we may stuff our lives full, when we fail to attend to our deeper calling we often go unsatisfied.

In this state, life can feel like it is spinning out of control. You are constantly doing more, going faster and racing on the treadmill of life. It may feel like you are taking on more and more yet achieving less and less. Many of us are constantly busy. Going, doing and staying occupied with lots of little tasks. But how often do you step back and look at the larger picture?

Finding a stillness within the chaos can be the key to pondering the larger meaning of your life. There is a Zen story that says that the best way to clear a glass of dirty, cloudy water is to let it be. Allow it to rest in stillness, without touching it for a time. This same principle holds true in your life. The mind and soul need quiet time to settle and be able to recognize what is truly important. In this stillness, it is easier to separate the chaos, noise and fury of the outside world from our inner longings, thoughts and desires.

It can be helpful to look beyond the busyness of your daily activities and focus on the essence and stillness that you can find as you slow down and reflect inward. In a busy life, this can seem challenging. As you are running around trying to accomplish everything, you get caught up in traffic, miss the train or are running late for your meeting. As soon as one meeting ends, you rush off to your next appointment. You can feel frazzled and pulled out of the present into past worries or future anxieties.

It can seem hard to find the present moment and even more difficult to remain there. We are often so rushed while striving to squeeze in so many tasks that we fail to slow down and reflect on what is actually occurring in our lives. This lack of mindfulness and failure to reflect on what all of this truly means creates a constant state of chaos in the mind, body and spirit. You can begin to lack awareness and presence.

Fortunately, the calm, insight and ease of the present is always accessible to you. You have the power to take intentional steps to move away from constant doing to rest into simply being. As you are able to settle into the calm of the present and find a way out of distractions, superficial obsessions and constant thinking, you are able to move forward with a clearer vision and sense of purpose. This allows you to more effectively focus your energy and make decisions which are aligned with your core desires and values.

"Breathing in, I calm body and mind. Breathing out, I smile. Dwelling in the present moment I know this is the only moment."
-Thich Nhat Hanh

The truth is that there is an underlying fullness, satisfaction and abundance which already exists. It is found in the present. Joy, love, happiness and dedication have intrinsic value that arise from the experiences themselves. When you fill up your life with conditions like these that have intrinsic value your heart is filled, and you are truly satisfied. You no longer need to over-schedule your life or work harder and faster to try to feel a sense of accomplishment. The key is learning to slow down and remain still enough in the present moment to be able to recognize this true peace, pleasure and fulfillment.

Cultivating a nonjudgmental awareness of the present bestows a host of benefits. Becoming more mindful of the way you feel physically, the balance of your emotions and the way you behave can have profound impacts on your health and wellbeing. In the chaotic scattered state of always going and doing, the brain reacts with a stress response which leads to a flood of hormones like cortisol and epinephrine (adrenaline) in your body. These chemicals are great when you need to run away from true danger or fight off a genuine foe, but they are not supportive of intuitive, insightful thinking or calm problem solving.

When you learn to still your mind and exist in the peace of the present, you can balance these hormones and allow the body and brain to function more optimally. This mindfulness reduces stress, boosts immune functioning, reduces chronic pain, lowers blood pressure and helps reduce the risk of many chronic diseases.

When you cultivate mindfulness, you can rest in the present and welcome this truth that everything which you need is already available to you. You are able to tap into the peace that comes from knowing that you are already complete, calm, happy and loved. You no longer crave something outside of you to fulfill your needs nor engage in strategies that distract from your true path. Your bucket is already full!

"The right word may be effective, but no word was ever as effective as a rightly timed pause."
-Mark Twain

As you find greater stillness, the chaos settles. You can slow down and see more clearly through the convoluted beliefs which you previously accepted. You can observe that you are essentially safe and sufficient in this instant right now. Notice that when you let go of this moment, another emerges. The potential is endlessly renewed and open for you to create.

In this calm stillness, you will sense that you are connected with all existence. Life flows. As you recognize your core truth, your authentic purpose becomes more distinct. The chaos calms, and you feel less driven to have to keep up with outside demands. From this place, you notice that you already have most, if not all, of what matters most.

Cultivating this mindfulness and accepting the abundance of the present does not mean giving up effort nor failing to have goals for the future. Instead it allows you to surrender the struggle and to lean into life with passionate purpose. You come to the realization that it is unnecessary to fight to survive. Instead you embrace the ease and flow of life that allow you to thrive!

PRESCRIPTION: MINDFULLY RESTING IN STILLNESS

You can practice cultivating a relaxation response, finding tranquility and enhancing mindfulness both formally and informally in your daily life. Exercises as simple as sitting and doing nothing, detaching from your thoughts and just letting the mind be as you rest naturally in the present moment can help you heal, clear and calm the mind.

This type of experience allows you to step out of the busyness, the doing and the achieving of daily life and permit yourself to focus inward and simply be present. Through such experiences, you cultivate the ability to step away from the constant chatter and occupation of your mind.

Mindfulness Meditation is an active form of meditation and self-awareness which involves focusing nonjudgmental attention on the moment at hand. Mindfulness-based meditation has been shown to reduce symptoms of depression and anxiety as effectively as some pharmaceutical drugs without the potential harmful side effects. Mindfulness can also profoundly change your approach to nourishing and appreciating your body.

Use this prescription to bring mindfulness into your daily life and cultivate a natural relaxation response. A mindfulness practice can be a great way to learn to slow down and calm the mind. You do not need to do anything fancy to take a five-minute vacation—just sit comfortably and move your focus inward. Incorporating even small amounts of meditation into your day can train your mind and body to relax and find calm.

Try practicing this exercise for five to ten minutes in the morning as you start your day and for five to ten minutes each evening to help you wind down and prepare for sleep. Find a quiet place and time where you will not be disturbed. Sit comfortably and close your eyes. Place your hands on your knees with your palms facing up to open your awareness or facing down to calm the mind.

Begin by taking some deep breaths. Inhale through your nose, and exhale through the mouth. Allow the air to flow in and fill your lungs and flow out as you relax with each exhale. Release tension, and allow yourself to be still in the present moment. As you breathe, begin to contemplate the source and flow of your breath: Where is your breath coming from? How is it moving through you? Feel the flow and tidal rhythm of the breath.

Bring your awareness to rest on your breath. If your attention wanders or thoughts are flooding your mind with chatter, do not become concerned. Gently note this experience, and simply bring your attention back to your breath. If you find yourself becoming anxious with thoughts, try journaling about your worries before you meditate to help decrease stress.

Engage in this practice daily, and notice how it impacts your sleep, mood and other aspects of your health. As you repeatedly practice relaxing your mind and surrendering to the stillness of the present moment, you will condition your mind to embrace the peace of simply being.

You can use this simple practice to recharge your mind, body and spirit. As you become more familiar with this place of stillness, a calm existence will become more natural. You will be able to tap into the peace and awareness which this centered state brings at any time.

PRESCRIPTION: BASKING IN YOUR PEACEFUL AWARENESS

Find a quiet place and time where you will not be disturbed. Sit or lie down comfortably and close your eyes. If you are lying down, you can use blankets and/or bolsters to support your body as needed.

Allow yourself to be curious during this practice. Remain open to accepting all that you experience. Welcome each thought, sensation, emotion and event as a wise messenger. Find the insight and guidance that they offer, and allow them to support you in cultivating a greater understanding of yourself and your path.

Begin by taking some deep breaths. Feel the coolness of the air flowing in and the warmth of the air as it leaves your body. Allow the air to flow in and fill your lungs and flow out as you relax with each exhale. Release tension, and allow yourself to be still in the present moment. Feel ease spreading throughout your body and mind.

Open your senses. Become aware of sounds in your environment. Notice the soft flow of your breath as it moves in and out. Welcome the sensation of your clothing, the floor and the air against your skin. Notice any sensations within your body. Allow any tension to melt away with your breath. Appreciate any smells and tastes. Bring your awareness to the experience of color and light.

Scan your body. Notice any tingling, tension, coolness or other sensations in your toes and feet. Welcome sensation in your calves and shins. Notice how your legs are resting against the ground. Sense your pelvis and hips. Notice the way they move softly with the breath. Welcome sensations in your abdomen, chest and back. Notice the expansion and contraction of the front and back body with each inhale and exhale. Sense your body breathing itself.

Notice the gentle pulsation of your heart. Feel and be the current and rhythm, the vibrant energy flowing throughout your body. Sense your shoulders and neck. Notice any tension or tightness, and let it melt away. Notice your arms, elbows, hands and fingers.

Feel the gentle air against your skin. Welcome the cool air against your forehead and cheeks. Notice how your tongue rests against your teeth. Feel your lips and throat. Become aware of your ears and the sounds you perceive. Feel your scalp and hair. Notice the way your head rests softly.

Allow yourself to feel any emotions within you. Note worry, sadness, joy, irritation, happiness, serenity and tension. Notice each just as they are in your body, and invite in calming peace and ease. Note and welcome memories, thoughts and images as they spontaneously unfold in your mind's eye. Without a need to judge or strive to control them, just allow them to be. Welcome the experience just as it is in its fullness.

Feel a sense of joy and bliss radiating from your heart. Allow this glowing wellbeing to spread throughout your entire body. Feel the warmth and light emanating to your whole being. Bask in this sense of joy, and allow it to fill you. Your deepest nature is peace and wisdom. You naturally have ease, calm, contentment and intuition. Allow yourself to sink into your true nature.

Reflect on your intention for this time. Maybe it is to rest and relax or to explore a certain belief, emotion or sensation. Perhaps you are ready to get deeper in touch with your intuition. Whatever you desire, feel it fully, and welcome it with your entire being.

Feel ease and calm spread throughout your body and mind. In this place of stillness, allow your heart's deepest desire to come to the surface. Feel this thing that you cherish and want more than anything else, whether it be insight, health, peace of mind, a relationship or awakening. Imagine and experience this dream with your whole being as if it has already become a reality. Reflect on what this feels like, look like, sounds like, smells like, tastes like and is like for you. Affirm it with your entire body and mind.

Bring attention to your inner resources and strength. Get in touch with the wealth of assets already within you. Tap into the peace, security, power, wellbeing, insight and calm which you hold within. Imagine yourself secure and at ease as you are bathed in a glowing white protective light. Know that you have this security and ease with you always and can access this safety and wellbeing whenever you choose.

Accept you as the conscious observer of your thoughts, emotions, body and dreams. Feel the awareness you cultivate. Resolving to be spacious and open. Allow yourself to be awake and open to yourself and the process of life. Reflect on your journey. Affirm this feeling of awareness and ease that is always present. Remember that this peace underlies every circumstance. Imagine yourself tapping into this ease at any time, cultivating wellbeing and awareness as your experience is unfolding.

When you are ready, begin to reorient to your surroundings. Begin to gently wiggle your fingers and toes. Stretch slowly and naturally, waking up. As you are ready, open your eyes. Come fully back to your environment, alert and awake to your present. Feel gratitude for yourself and your practice. Feel renewed and strengthened. Notice your deepened sense of connection with the flow of life. Remember this place of peace and insight as you go forward.

PRESCRIPTION: MINDFUL NOURISHMENT

This exercise will help you to increase your mindfulness around eating and how you use food in your life. As you explore how food impacts your life, focus inward. Use these reflection exercises to identify how food truly influences you individually. As you uncover your patterns and become more mindful, you can evolve your diet and nourishment to truly match and fulfill your needs.

Practicing mindful eating can help you connect with your intuition and establish an instinctual way of eating. This will help you obtain and maintain your optimal weight, make eating more pleasurable and decrease guilt. As you more easily connect with the peaceful stillness available to you in the present, you will cultivate mindfulness in every area of your life. With time and practice, this mindful approach to nourishment will become second nature.

Use this guide to *Simple | Pure | Whole*™ *Nourishment and Mindful Eating*[1] to explore your eating habits and patterns while you build your mindfulness through simple habits.

---

[1] Learn more about mindful, intuitive eating with my virtual course *What to Eat? An eater's guide to conquering cravings and returning to intuitive eating*, available at www.JenniferWeinbergMD.com/eatersguide

Sit Down in a Calm Setting

Create a calm environment in which to enjoy your meals. Sit down at an uncluttered table. Avoid eating on the run, in the car, standing by the fridge or in front of the TV or computer.

Take a Few Deep Breaths Before Eating

Try starting each meal with some deep, calming breaths. Pause to become fully present in the moment. Notice the colors, textures and aromas of the food on your plate. Reflect on how that food made it to your plate and all the love and effort that went into your meal.

Practice Gratitude

Before taking your first bite, take a moment to reflect on how grateful you are to have this nourishing and delicious food available to you. Express gratitude in whatever way feels meaningful to you.

Chew Well and Slowly

Chew your food slowly. As you break down the food, concentrate on the taste and texture.

Savor Flavor and Texture

Pay attention to the flavors, crunchiness, creaminess and temperature of what you are eating.

Set Down Your Fork Between Bites

Experiment with pausing between bites. Set down your fork, take a few deep breaths and relax. Notice how you feel before picking it up again. Check in with yourself and ask, Am I full? Am I thirsty? Do I feel satisfied by this food?

Eat When Hungry, Stop When Full

Try to notice what triggers you to reach for food. Before mindlessly grabbing for a snack or meal, ask yourself, Am I really hungry for food? Am I hungry for something else? Is this the best option and quality of food available to me? As you eat, notice when you are comfortably but not overly full and stop eating at that point. You want to feel satisfied but not stuffed.

Take some time to reflect on what triggers you to eat. Think about these questions:

- What triggers you to eat?
- Is there something in your environment, a situation, a person and/or an emotion that triggers eating?
- Can you create a new reaction pattern to prompts which are not based in true hunger?
- How can you cope with emotional triggers?

PRESCRIPTION: WELCOME THE PAUSE

To begin to slow down and cultivate mindfulness and awareness of the moments of your life, there are some powerful steps you can take. In order to prevent crashing and spiraling out of control, it is necessary to know how to apply the brakes, to be able to pause. In daily life, pausing gives you the gift of time. Time to calm down, find stillness, sort out your priorities, tap into your intuition, truly connect with yourself and others and respond to life from a centered place of wisdom.

"Those who are wise won't be busy, and those who are too busy can't be wise."
-Lin Yutang

Use this prescription to permit yourself to slow down and welcome the pause. Allow yourself to not always act and do. Give yourself permission to slow down and simply be from time to time. During your day, find breaks, and stop for even a few moments. Tune into your emotions, what is going on in your mind, how you feel deep inside. Pause and create space for your true experience to occur. Use this momentarily deepened awareness to catch up with yourself.

Begin by tuning into your breath whenever you feel frazzled, rushed or chaotic. It may seem counterintuitive to slow down when you feel pressured to get more and more accomplished, but enhancing your presence will help you be present and truly absorb the moment more fully. Attune to the breath, your body and your surroundings. Be present for the task at hand. This will help you remain more grounded in the present moment.

For example, if you are in your seventh meeting of the day and thinking of what happened in the last meeting and how you are going to get dinner on the table in between picking up the kids and cleaning up the house, take a moment to center yourself, focus on your breath, look people in the eye and truly listen.

Effective communication requires a high level of self-awareness. When you make a conscious effort to be centered in yourself and aware of the present moment, you can move beyond just hearing the words that the other person is saying and begin to try to comprehend the complete message being communicated. When you slow down and remain present, you can put aside distracting thoughts of the past and future, truly connect with the other person and respond openly, thoughtfully and respectfully. Notice how the pause changes your reaction and the other person's response to you. In this way you will build rapport, trust and engagement.

It is also helpful to leave time in your schedule to soak in life and reflect on what is occurring. Take the time to savor the flavors, aromas and textures of your meal, and you will find that you more fully recognize your true hunger and satiety levels. Leave time for reflecting on what you just worked on or accomplished as you go about your day.

Ask yourself if the experience was rewarding? Were your needs met? Was the interaction fulfilling? Taking these moments for reflection may mean pausing a few minutes as you sit in the car before driving away or mindfully embracing a loved one and pausing to acknowledge the moment and connection.

"In stillness the world is restored."
- Lao Tzu

Use this prescription to cultivate a habit of slowing down and becoming more mindful of your presence. Welcome the pause from doing, and enjoy leaning into being.

PRESCRIPTION: NATURAL CONNECTIONS

Finding harmony with nature helps balance hormones, relax the body, calm the mind, ease anxiety, enhance focus and sharpen intuition. Spending time in nature is a great way to cultivate stillness and deepen your connection with the natural ease and flow of life. As you get outdoors immersed in the natural world, you escape the chaos and distractions of the modern world. Your focus returns to the present moment in which you are alive.

Use this prescription to commit to spending more time in nature. Take a walk by the edge of the ocean, hike up a mountain, sit quietly in the forest, practice yoga by the lake, walk barefoot in the grass or sit by a bubbling brook. Find your favorite spot where you can connect with the natural world, and simply allow yourself to soak it all in. See how many beautiful reasons there are for you to smile. Be grateful for the sounds, sights, aromas and sensations you are experiencing.

Try a walking meditation in nature. Start your walk in silence with an intention of appreciation—appreciation for your body's ability to walk and carry you through life, appreciation for what is scenic around you, appreciation for what is beautiful in your life on this day. Notice each step you take, one after another. Pay attention to the physical act of walking. Allow yourself to let go of all concern for the past and future and to rest in the awareness of the present.

Discover at least one new plant, view or creature in your surroundings that you have not noticed before. Soak in that experience and notice all aspects of what you find. Make a point of stopping along the way to appreciate everything existing with you here in this world. Cultivate your intention to appreciate our sacred planet, and connect with the beauty of the natural world. Notice the elements of the earth, sky, water, fire and wind. Appreciate how these elements organize and interact to create and support life.

"Adopt the pace of nature; her secret is patience."
-Ralph Waldo Emerson

Make a conscious effort this week to carry the peace and stillness you find when you spend time in nature with you into your everyday life. Whenever possible, strive to find your natural state. Physically and mentally tap into the rhythms of nature and the ease and flow they bring.

Become more aware of the natural ebb and flow of nature's cycles. Each of your cells has an internal clock which is linked to the rhythms of nature. When you ignore this connection, life can become imbalanced and cause struggle. However, when these are in sync, your life has greater balance and vitality.

To align yourself with the natural rhythms of the world, try awakening at or before sunrise. Engage is gentle morning exercise before 10am, during this time when physical strength naturally increases. In the midday, the sun is highest in the sky and the day is at its hottest. Try eating your largest meal between 10am and 2pm, and notice how this feels for you. Focus on locally sourced, seasonal foods to remain in sync with your surroundings. During the natural stillness of the evening between 5pm and 6pm, take the opportunity to meditate, still the mind and relax, even if it is only for a few minutes. To close the day, start settling down and quieting the mind as early in the evening as possible. Consider journaling, reading, taking a relaxing bath or gently stretching. Try to get to sleep before 10pm to allow your body to renew, detoxify and reset.

Follow these natural guidelines for a few days and notice how your body, mind and spirit reacts. As you settle into a natural rhythm, you will find that the body naturally tends to sync with these cycles.

"I go to nature to be soothed and healed, and to have my senses put in order."
-John Burroughs

Clear out the clutter in your home and bring a touch of nature into your space. Create a sacred area to honor the beauty, abundance and rhythms of the natural world. Intentionally choose and place natural objects there that call out to you.

Practice a blessing and reflection of gratitude for the earth. Thank the earth for providing nourishing food to feed your body. Thank the sun for warming your skin and lighting the world. Thank the trees for providing shelter and filtering the air that you breathe. Thank the water for nurturing your cells. Express gratitude for the opportunity to share in the wonder that is life.

CHAPTER 7: A Grateful Opening to Hope and Faith

OFTEN, WE CAN GET CAUGHT up in the day-to-day grind and commotion of our lives. Your life may be so full of obligations, tasks and possessions yet empty of true meaning and passion. You can stay so busy running from one task to another and trying to finally feel accomplished enough or satisfied with your life that your genuine passions and dreams get pushed aside. You may feel a sense of longing for something bigger or more aligned with your authentic self, yet stay busy satisfying your everyday needs and cravings.

It can be easy to settle for a belief that you do not deserve more or that some things are simply unattainable. Perhaps you look at others and think that opportunities and gifts come so much easier for them. Sometimes it can be difficult to recognize your gifts or allow yourself to accept your big dreams. But you can create and live a life that you appreciate and adore!

"Happiness is as a butterfly which, when pursued, is always beyond our grasp, but which if you will sit down quietly, may alight upon you."
-Nathaniel Hawthorne

Gratitude encompasses an appreciation for the circumstances, material things, experiences and people in your life. It also involves faith, hope and trust. You may be grateful for the abundance in your life and your ability to make your own decisions in alignment with your authentic path. You may appreciate the knowledge, skills, passions and strengths which you have that allow you to create the life of your dreams. You may express gratitude for your gifts and confidence and the vitality that comes when you are living your life in alignment with your essential self.

Expressing gratitude brings magic into our lives. No matter what is going on or however chaotic life may seem at the moment, there is always something for which to be grateful. When you focus on aspects of your life and moments that evoke joy, happiness and gratitude, you generate an energy of creation, forward movement and positivity. You are reprogramming your subconscious mind and rewiring your brain with new neural pathways. This is the key to creating new vitality and momentum in your life, breaking old habits and manifesting your authentic and passionate life.

"If the only prayer you ever said in your whole life was 'Thank you,'
that would suffice."
-Meister Eckhart

Appreciating what you have at any given moment helps you remember and celebrate the present. It also focuses your thoughts, and therefore your energy, on the positive. When you cultivate an intention to ignite gratitude within you, you create abundance and can receive more openly all the treasures which life has to offer. By giving thanks instead of grasping for more, you are able to receive more freely.

Gratitude enhances the value you extract from your life experiences. When you appreciate an event, you are less likely to take it for granted. As you notice and celebrate the positives in your life, your pleasure is magnified and you more deeply participate in creating an authentic life. It is easier to be satisfied with life when you recognize all that you already have. This helps you step out of the constant struggle to have more material possessions or shop to fill an emotional void.

Cultivating daily gratitude expands your perspective and reminds you of the richness which already exists in your life. Instead of simply watching life happen or being an observer to outside events, you more fully engage in your life as you recognize all that is flowing well.

Focusing on gratitude cultivates positivity in your life and enhances self-worth. As you feel grateful, you drown out negativity, jealousy, envy, regret, resentment and depression. By overcoming these negative emotions, you open up space for true happiness and a joyful experience of life. You cannot embrace gratitude and resentment at the same time, so expressing gratitude changes the way you relate to the world.

As you cultivate a grateful disposition, you shift your perspective. Those who have a regular practice of recognizing how the world is working for them instead of against them are more confident and resilient. A person with a grateful perspective can recover more quickly from daily stresses as well as serious adversity, trauma and suffering. A grateful attitude shifts how you interpret life events and guards against spiraling into anxiety, post-traumatic stress, obsession and negativity.

"Your attitude colors every aspect of your life. It is like the mind's paintbrush. It can paint everything in bright, vibrant colours, creating a masterpiece. Or it can make everything dark and dreary."
-J. Maxwell

Everything in the universe is energy. Our attention and thoughts carry energy and influence our life experience in a myriad of ways. Our lives are formed by what we notice and infuse with focus and energy. You choose what to pay attention to. By focusing attention on that which is good in your life—prosperity, creativity, joy, wellbeing, love, exuberance, passion, awe—you draw more energy to the creation of these aspects of your life. You begin to notice more things you appreciate, and a sense of abundance grows. A heart-centered gratitude practice opens you up to a deeper awareness of who you truly are and leads to greater alignment with your authentic passionate life!

Studies show that regularly focusing on gratitude enhances alertness, enthusiasm, determination, attentiveness and energy. These qualities strengthen your capacity for achieving the things you truly want in life. Similarly, research demonstrates that people who consistently practice gratitude have improved health, stronger immune systems, less pain, lower blood pressure, more refreshing sleep, greater optimism and less loneliness. When you embrace these positive attributes, you align more closely with your authentic purpose, add greater value to the world and cultivate prosperity!

PRESCRIPTION: GRATITUDE IN EVERY MOMENT

When you focus on the aspects of life for which you are grateful, you open up to accepting life as it is. You are able to more serenely relax into the flow of life and appreciate the present moment. As you consciously and intentionally focus your attention on developing gratitude, you see simple gifts in life as exciting and energizing. You will come to experience life in a more engaged and rewarding way. Spending even a little time each day reflecting on those things which you appreciate can powerfully impact your mood, health and life!

"Every day I see or hear something that more or less kills me with delight."
-Mary Oliver

Set aside some time each day to reflect and cultivate gratitude. For some, first thing in the morning upon waking works well. Others prefer to reflect on each day's gifts at the close of the day.

Write down some things you are grateful for in each day. They do not have to be complicated or spectacular. There is no right or wrong choice. It could be your dog snoring on the couch, the sunlight streaming in through the window, the subtle aroma of the roses blooming outside of your window, an embrace from a loved one or the warm, cozy socks keeping your feet warm. Just get in touch with whatever fills your heart with gratitude in that moment.

Write down the aspects of life for which you are grateful. It can be powerful to put the pen to paper and document what you are experiencing.

- Think of someone towards whom you feel gratitude. What about this person makes you grateful?
- Take an inventory of the things in your life for which you are grateful. What events in your life bring you feelings of gratitude?
- List some gifts of the natural world for which you are grateful.
- Think about some qualities within yourself for which you are grateful.
- How can you celebrate the many gifts you have in your life each day? In what way can you honor and recognize those things for which you are grateful in your life?

PRESCRIPTION: GRATITUDE IS ALL AROUND ME

Taking just a few minutes each day to focus on gratitude can build a powerful habit over time. As you cultivate a practice of recognizing all that is good in life, you will find greater gifts and opportunities to appreciate. Use this guided meditation to boost your gratitude practice and remind yourself of all the wonderful gifts you have received.

Sit comfortably and close your eyes. Bring your attention inward. Bring your full awareness to your body, and notice what is there. Relax any areas in which you are holding tension. Settle into a comfortable, relaxed position.

Be grateful for your body. You may have judged it in the past, degraded it or criticized it. But it is this body that has allowed you to experience life. It has carried you through with strength. Recognize its abilities and all that it does for you. Honor your body.

Be grateful for your eyes and the beauty they behold. Be grateful for the brilliant blue sky and glow of the sunrise.

Feel gratitude towards your ears that allow you to hear glorious music and the soft hush of the wind. Express appreciation for being able to hear the birds chirping at dawn and the crash of the waves against the shore.

Give thanks for your nose through which you perceive the sweet smell of a rose and the scent of the air after a spring rain.

Feel gratitude for your mouth, lips and tongue which allow you to make joyful music and express yourself verbally each day. Give thanks for being able to taste the sweetness of honey and the sharp tang of a lemon.

Appreciate your arms that allow you to embrace a loved one. Realize the beauty in a firm handshake and being able to pet an animal.

Acknowledge your legs which strongly carry you through life. Experience gratitude for the stability and mobility they provide.

Give thanks for your skin that allows you to feel a gentle touch and the warmth of the sun.

Feel gratitude for your breath as it flows in and out. This breath is always with you, refreshing your energy and sustaining your life. As you take a deep breath in feel how this breath fills you with light, energy and life. As you breathe out, release negativity and tension.

Appreciate the consistent beating of your heart. Notice its unceasing work to keep you alive and allow you to experience all that life provides. Be grateful for your heart.

Appreciate and give thanks for your whole body. For all that it is and does for you.

Now brings your awareness to your environment. Notice the roof over your head. Appreciate that it is keeping you dry and safe.

Feel grateful for the nourishment you have received. Remember the meals you have enjoyed and the strength they have provided.

Be grateful for the sun and the rain, the wind and the snow. Appreciate the freshness of a new day and the changing cycles of nature. Feel grateful for all that nature provides.

Now feel gratitude for those in your life and all that they have done for you and added to your existence. Express gratitude for loved ones, family, teachers, guides, friends, mentors, colleagues and pets. Appreciate their roles in your life and the impact they have. Embrace the connections you have cultivated and the ways in which your relationships nurture you. Feel grateful for the lessons and interactions you have had and how you have grown. Express gratitude for everyone who has cared for you, loved you and supported you.

Bring your awareness to this moment. Be grateful for the time, the space and the awareness you have right now. Take a deep breath, and allow a wave of glowing light and gratitude to wash over you. Feel the light of gratitude for all that you have received as it fills your body and flows out of your heart. Allow this gratitude to radiate into you. And feel this light flow from your heart back out into the world, forming a continuous cycle of positive, vibrant energy. Take some deep breaths and relax into this light. Feel it fully, and absorb its energy. Allow it to support and nurture you. Enjoy some time immersed in this sense of gratitude.

When you are ready, allow your awareness to broaden. Take some deep breaths, and slowly come back to your surroundings. Take the time that you need. When you are ready, open your eyes. Feel refreshed as you return to your day with a renewed sense of appreciation for all that you have and all that you are.

PRESCRIPTION: APPRECIATE BEAUTY

Beauty can be found in many aspects of our lives if we only take the time to look for it. You do not have to visit a tropical island or a museum to be in the presence of something beautiful. In fact, you can find beauty even in the small and simplest aspects of life. The sound of the rain against your roof. The curve of a blade of grass. The face of a dear friend. The touch of a soft sweater. The shine of a glass. The feeling of an embrace. There are so many things and experiences creating beauty all around us.

Where do you find beauty? When you start to deliberately look for beauty in the world you will begin to notice that it is everywhere. How do you feel when you experience something beautiful? Often, experiencing beauty, even in its small or commonplace forms, brings joy, encourages hope, relieves stress, lifts spirits, calms the mind and eases tension.

Take some time each day to open yourself to the beauty surrounding you. Look more mindfully at the world around you. Cultivate an enhanced awareness of the beauty in ordinary things and experiences which you may have otherwise overlooked. Notice the way the clouds drift along in the sky. Pay attention to the feeling of the grass beneath your feet. Listen more closely to the wind rustling through the tress. More mindfully taste the sweetness of ripe fruit. Hear the joy in friends laughing together. Notice the lovely aspects of aspirations and dreams.

As you go through your day, seek out beautiful sensations, feelings, encounters and ideas. Make note of where you find beauty in unexpected places. Allow yourself to be pleasantly surprised as you remain open to noticing lovely aspects of life outside of what you would traditionally think of as pretty or picturesque.

As you hunt for and find beauty all around you, remain open to receiving it. Feel it, and experience what it is like to be in its presence. Open your heart to a growing sense of boundless beauty in your life.

And realize the endless beauty that is also within you. Use this light and energy to generate greater beauty with your words, actions and intentions. Notice how this changes how you feel and what you create with your life!

PRESCRIPTION: STOP, DROP NEGATIVITY AND COUNT YOUR BLESSINGS

You have a choice to create positivity, love, generosity and respect with the energy you project into the world. You do not have to buy into or believe everything you think or become attached to all of the stories you tell yourself. Instead, you can cultivate a deeper awareness of your thoughts and emotions and the impact that they have on your life. As you develop a more mindful presence you are empowered to focus on the goodness within yourself, the beauty in humanity and the passion of life. The more you find the positive in life's circumstances, the more you can shed limiting belief systems and tap into the flow of an authentic life.

There are some useful strategies for releasing negative beliefs and limiting patterns. Start by committing to seek out the positive in each day. Give thanks for your blessings both large and small, and remain open to receiving the abundance which is there for you. Affirm that your life experience overall is supportive and pleasant. To reinforce this concept, take note of kind acts, meaningful connections and little miracles that take place. Focus on the goodness of life, and you will begin to notice more and more beauty within and around you.

Brainstorm a list of ways that you can step back and stop your emotions from taking over. This could include listening to your favorite music, practicing breathing exercises, stretching or practicing yoga, taking a walk outside, doing a mindfulness meditation, gardening, volunteering, creating art, reading poetry, talking to a friend, taking a hot bath or getting a massage.

Embrace those passions which you may have been pushing away or crowding out with unhealthy habits. Engage in art and other forms of self-expression that allow you to express that voice of doubt, fear, pain and trepidation. Acknowledge these feelings and release them. You may choose to journal, write yourself love notes, dance, sing, play music or otherwise express your inner voice. Anything that engages you in a healthy activity and encourages positive action can help you cope and process life.

Over time you will create a new pattern of reacting to stress, fear, sadness and other overwhelming emotions. Having constructive, realistic options for coping with life allows you to respond calmly and with self-awareness.

CHAPTER 8: Surrender to the Stillness and Have Faith in the Flow

YOU DETERMINE YOUR DESTINY and have the power to co-design your life with the universe as your guide. Your thoughts, intuition, actions, beliefs, passions and inactions shape your experience. You are an active participant in your life, but the journey does not have to be a struggle. If you open your heart and mind and maintain faith in your capabilities and the flow of your path, you will recognize the guidance, strength and wisdom which are within you and around you to support your movement through life.

"Everything in life is vibration."
-Albert Einstein

Finding stillness and learning to sit in the present moment allow you to connect with the natural flow and momentum of life. As you surrender and trust that everything is happening in the perfect time and way, you allow for good things to happen for you and support the creation of your authentic life. You begin to recognize that those little coincidences and synchronicities are cues to guide you along your path and encouragements to help you remain resilient.

It is not necessary to strive, struggle or plead with a higher force to bring you more. Your job is to put your faith in the process, trust and devote yourself to your passionate purpose with joy and enthusiasm. This creates an environment for receiving and accepting what you know and believe you are worthy of experiencing.

As you open yourself to the stillness of the moment and have faith in the flow of life, you deepen your connection to your authentic self and awaken to an abundant life. By cultivating consciousness and presence during ordinary moments, you become more fully alive and aligned with your passionate purpose. This profound presence is available in the gentle flow of each breath and in the stillness beyond the struggle.

Let Go and Ride Waves of Adversity

Life is full of surprises. Sometimes things are difficult. A hurricane destroys your community. Your flight gets cancelled. A relationship loses its spark. The company where you have worked for over twenty years goes bankrupt. Everything you have built your life around seems pulled out from under you in a moment. The chaos, unease, panic and disappointment can be overwhelming.

There are inevitably going to be times in our lives when things just do not go according to the plan. This may involve extreme shifts, such as a natural disaster, or smaller yet still disruptive experiences, like moving across the country. Sometimes, we are let down and feel unsettled when we are disappointed or an expected experience does not go as planned. Other times, life may hit us hard, shattering our current understanding of the world.

Life does present unavoidable difficulties. How do you react when your expectations are not met or things do not unfold as you had anticipated? Do you cope with randomness in life by becoming overwhelmed or caught up in the chaos? Or do you calmly ride out the storm?

The difference between emotional upheaval and steady resilience in the face of unexpected events often depends on our ability to transcend the inconsistency and chaos of life. This approach is not meant to minimize the impacts of adversity in life or to suggest that you should give up trying to improve things. Instead it is about leaning into the flow and surrendering the struggle.

So often we add unnecessary anxiety, fear, frustration, self-doubt, insecurity and aggravation to our circumstances by resisting challenges and difficulties. Life unfolds with greater ease when you allow your experience to be separate from uncontrollable occurrences and outcomes. You can cultivate a greater state of calm and consistency amongst life's unexpected chaos through building awareness, mindfulness and transcendence.

In the moment, try accepting the struggle. Acknowledge the anxiety, frustration, fear, pain, stress, conflict and panic. Attempt to step back and observe what is happening without becoming attached. Approach adversity with compassion and a peaceful resolve to address the circumstances without struggling or resisting. Avoid blame. Do not forget to appreciate those things which are not difficult at the time, those situations which flow with ease.

When you are able to connect with your inner compassionate presence, you can remain in the present moment without getting caught up in judgment, anger and reaction. Celebrate the transformation that occurs through experience. Appreciate the facts of life—impermanence, interdependence, momentum, flow. Express gratitude for your sources of strength and support, both internal and external. Honor yourself for your resilience.

When you are able to transcend the realm of relativity where randomness is frequent, you can access a deeper level of awareness. This is often referred to as Pure Consciousness and allows you to be aware of the present yet not stuck in the future or the past, the good or the bad, the expected or the inconsistent. When you work to find this place through practices like yoga, meditation and mindfulness, you can strengthen your connection with a deeper level of life. You can find a natural place of calm and consistency.

As you cultivate an awareness of the ease and flow of life, you will find yourself able to remain in this place of peace more and more. Over time, you will be able to more easily remain separate from the randomness around you. It is like being immersed in the deeper layer of the ocean that is calm and still even when the surface is constantly changing, turbulent and choppy. In this way, you can exist amongst the chaos of life on the surface, yet simultaneously remain calm, centered and non-reactive at a deeper, inner level.

When you face a challenge or dilemma or feel stuck, your first instinct may be to become overwhelmed, withdraw or panic. But these chaotic reactions will only add fuel to the fire. In this unsettled state, your mind and perspective is clouded. Amidst this reactionary stance, you are prevented from hearing your inner wisdom and knowing the true solutions. Often, the non-stop chatter in your mind can create perceived illusions of confusion and disorder.

Have Faith in the Flow

Alternatively, when you surrender to the situation that is making you feel frustrated, overwhelmed or stuck, you settle into the flow. Often people spend their time doing one thing after another. We work longer and harder, multitask, accumulate more possessions and stay so busy that sometimes life just flies by. We become so fixated on doing more and more but often fail to bring much intuition and awareness to the process.

Without this insight, you may feel depleted from grinding through repetitive tasks, racing from one meeting to the next, worrying about getting everything accomplished and drowning in an overflowing inbox. The doing can seem mechanical, and you can become numb to true meaning. The relentless pace and stress can wear you down mentally and physically.

We can forget that everything in the universe is connected by the flow of energy. Life is an ever expanding flow of potential, a stream of endless possibilities. But we often fail to realize these opportunities when we get stuck in our day-to-day responsibilities and tasks.

Conversely, when you are in sync with the flow of everyday activities and acting in accordance with your authentic purpose, you find pleasure in using your talents and capabilities. You relish the unity and continuity of existence and find fulfillment in connecting with and helping others.

When faced with difficulties, whether big or small, reflect on your strength, support and faith. Faith involves a sense of trusting and having confidence in something. It includes assumptions and expectations and evolves from direct experience, a deep sense of knowing and reason.

> *"Faith is taking the first step even when you don't see the whole staircase."*
> *-Martin Luther King, Jr.*

Faith can involve religion but also a more general sense of believing and entrusting. When we affirm our faith in the world, we are grounded in a more peaceful, secure existence. This trusting gives us a visceral sense of conviction and helps us integrate logic, emotion and awakening in an efficient manner.

When you have faith in life, you surrender to the flow and are strengthened and supported. The world is less scary, and you are more easily able to overcome fear and doubt. As you strengthen your faith, you cultivate optimism and hope and put forth action that leads to results which confirm your faith in a reinforcing positive cycle.

As you bring greater mindfulness to your life and slow down, you will feel more relaxed and at ease. Cultivating a sustained moment-to-moment awareness gives you a continuity of presence and focus. With this approach, doing can become a part of living that brings fulfillment instead of a rushed, chaotic battle. Use the opportunity in simple activities to find mindful presence. Notice the peace and freedom this brings.

The essence of finding this peace rests in putting your faith in the flow. When you are at ease to do freely and with trust that everything is unfolding just as it should, you are not trapped, stressed or contracted. From a more grounded place of calm, you more easily trust your intuition and surrender to the guidance within and all around you. Instead of reacting and adding to the pandemonium, practice surrendering. Find stillness. Trust. Allow everything to flow in just the way it is meant to unfold.

Ride the Wave and Get Unstuck

Amidst the race to accomplish more and go faster, it is easy to get stuck. You may feel paralyzed by a decision, stuck in resentment, unable to forgive, unsure about how to create your future or trapped in a destructive, repetitive pattern. When you are stuck, your life feels entrenched, hopeless, insecure and empty.

Fortunately, you can become unstuck by shifting your perception and discovering new insights and attitudes. Instead of becoming caught up in chaos or trying to distract yourself from negative thoughts, allow yourself to fully experience your feelings and let them go. Surrendering to experiences does not mean giving up or endorsing a situation. Instead, it involves completely accepting the moment as it is and making peace with that. Your emotions will naturally become unstuck, and life can flow peacefully.

Instead of resisting negative emotions and creating greater stress from fighting what you find uncomfortable, you can recognize, embrace and let go of such feelings. Moving away from resistance to your feelings allows negativity to be released instead of becoming stuck in the body.

When you choose to remain calm and ride the waves of life instead of fighting them, you create a peaceful, centered and conscious awareness. It is not necessary to struggle. It is simply enough to be aware, mindful and present. Bringing your energy to the present moment allows you to quiet your mind, open your heart and get unstuck. You cannot change the past, but you can choose your perception and interpretation of what those experiences mean. This determines what level of happiness, peace and fulfillment you receive moving forward.

"The future is completely open, and we are writing it moment to moment."
-Pema Chodron

As you become more connected with the flow of the universe, you can manifest more ease in your life. Explore where you may be failing to surrender in your life. What are you fighting against or resisting? What would it look like if you let go and leaned into your experience? What would freedom feel like for you? Cultivate your awareness as you create a meaningful future.

When you give yourself permission to celebrate this transformation, you are able to embrace the momentum and motion in your life as you embark on your authentic journey. Honor your unique path and pace. You have the courage to create new beginnings, growth and abundant flow as you step into the next phase of your life, one that you select and create. Choose to cultivate your connection to the natural flow of life, and invite an ease and peace into your existence.

Remember, you are always supported. All you need to do is remain calm, centered and open to following the guidance. This will help you remain in the ease and flow of life and become empowered to reach your passionate purpose!

PRESCRIPTION: FIND GRATITUDE AND FAITH AMID TURMOIL

When the unexpected strikes or things do not go as you had envisioned, it is easy to get caught up in emotional chaos. It may seem hard to look at the bright side when you are faced with tragedy, frustration and misfortune, but there is always something to be thankful for, even in the darkest of situations.

It may not seem obvious or easy to find right away, but when you look deeper and shift your focus away from the negative and towards the positive, you can find peace through an attitude of compassion and gratitude. Be thankful for what you do have amidst loss. Be grateful for your life and potential. Look at what is going right.

Even when you are frustrated, panic-stricken, angry, disappointed or overwhelmed, remember to be kind. Show compassion for yourself and those around you. Instead of reacting with loud or violent emotions, remain calm and supportive. Search for ways to help those around you. Show small acts of kindness that create a ripple of love and gratitude.

Use this prescription to cultivate a mindful stillness amidst everyday challenges. Start noticing how both your inner world and outer world are constantly evolving. Pay attention to how your thoughts and feelings, tasks, physical being and circumstances shift. Know that suffering is only temporary and that the present is the only true constant. Appreciate how these evolving circumstances allow things to arise and recede due to many causes. Feel the flow of life like a moving river as reality emerges and evolves. Work on seeing challenges as opportunities for learning, growth and cultivating faith.

- What do you have faith in? Make a list of what you have faith in, both inside of yourself and out in the universe.
- What does it feel like to trust in this faith?
- How does your faith support you?
- How can you strengthen your beliefs in your own resilience to reinforce your faith in yourself?
- Think about any areas of your life where your faith is lacking or misplaced. Where in your life could you use more trust, security and conviction?

Brainstorm about missed opportunities for trusting in your own strengths, other people and the universe. Where could you reasonably place greater faith? Consciously choose at least one of these in which to believe. Place a reminder of your conviction somewhere you will see it often during the day. Remember your reasons for relying upon it, and imagine how you will benefit as you place more trust in this situation, virtue or person.

PRESCRIPTION: BE STILL IN THE PRESENT MOMENT

Our lives are busy, packed with responsibilities, obligations, activities and interactions. When the unexpected occurs or we are frustrated and disappointed with our life circumstances, we can get caught up in future worries or hung up in the past. We can become anxious about the what, how, when and why of our circumstances. It is easy to lose touch with the present moment amid the chaos.

Instead, choose to be still. Each moment offers you the opportunity to open your heart to love, hope, forgiveness, peace and joy. Practice bringing your awareness to the present moment. Keep your attention on the now. As you find ways to be present and accept the current circumstances, your mind can find stillness and escape from the chaos instead of joining in. Even when life does not make sense, the more you are able to remain calm and centered, the better equipped you will be to weather the storm and understand what the challenge can teach you.

You can use this simple yet powerful exercise to lower your stress, enhance resiliency, improve focus and strengthen your ability to flow with life and be still in the present moment.

Find a quiet place and time where you will not be disturbed. Sit comfortably and close your eyes. Begin by taking some deep breaths. Allow the air to flow in and fill your lungs and flow out as you relax with each exhale. Release tension, and allow yourself to be still in the present moment.

Focus your attention around and in your heart. Feel a glowing, healing, white light beginning to arise and grow. Feel this warm radiance around your heart. As you breathe, imagine that your breath is flowing in and out from your heart. Allow the light to expand and fill you up as you inhale into your heart. As you breathe in, allow this light to flood into you and fill you with a warm, loving glow.

Allow the light to move into your feet and fill your legs with love. Feel the light soaking into every part of your being. Bring this healing presence to all the points of your body, filling you up with peaceful light. As you become saturated and bathed in this tender radiance, feel yourself filling with hope, comfort, security and delight.

Imagine radiating this positive energy from your heart as you exhale. Allow this light to radiate from your heart, connecting you with an endless flow of light and love that is all around you. As you calmly inhale and exhale, observe this unending cycle of positive energy. Take a deep breath and feel yourself surrounded by supportive, glowing white light. Rest in the glow which fills you and surrounds you. Let go, and relax into the support you receive in this presence. Release any thoughts, emotions or reactions. Allow them to melt away as you simply breathe in and out, relaxing into the gentle wave of the breath.

Try this exercise several times each day. Find opportunities to open your heart and replicate this feeling of openness, flow and stillness. Know that this security and serenity is there for you at all times.

PRESCRIPTION: BORN FREE

You were born into this world with all the tools, strengths, passions and wisdom that you need. As you entered this world with an open heart, you were full of light and love. This innocence and hope allowed you to delight in small and simple things. You saw the world with fresh, unbiased eyes. You had yet to build up the layers of armor to protect yourself from threats you perceived in the world nor shaped yourself to strive to be something you thought you ought to be.

Remember now your newly born spirit. Recall the freedom and innocence of this time. Feel yourself with an open heart, filled with light and love. Here in the present moment, reconnect with this innocence and hope. Imagine what it was like to discover new things with fresh eyes. See the way you can approach the world with delight. Allow yourself to fall in love with small details, and experience the fullness you find.

Think about your dreams and passions. Make a list of those dreams, passions and delights that you desire in your life. It is never too late to elicit your authentic desires.

- What has filled you with enthusiasm and zest for life since you were young?
- What is it that you have cherished for your entire life?

Reflect on your life.

- When have you realized that things were flowing smoothly and with ease?
- What did it feel like when everything just felt right and you knew you were on your true path?

Notice how the universe sends you signals that you are in sync with life. Perhaps people have showed up unexpectedly offering just what you needed at that time, whether it be support, advice, a new job opportunity, friendship or other forms of inspiration. Maybe you recall moments when your intuition, thoughts and gut feelings have provided reassurance that you were on the right path or making the right choice. Possibly you have noticed signs and clues that have allowed you to know something before it happened.

Remember how you have been guided towards that which gives your life true meaning, purpose and value. Keep these experiences in mind. Recall the strength and determination you receive as you surrender to the flow and embrace the momentum with intention and faith.

PRESCRIPTION: LET GO OF NEGATIVE EMOTIONS

Sometimes we can become caught up in feelings of anger, fear, sadness, disappointment, frustration and hurt. Exploring negative emotions and thoughts in a specific way can help us move beyond this negativity and get 'unstuck.'

Try this meditation technique to vanquish negativity and calm the body and mind. Use this practice as a way to let go of thoughts and become more aware of the present moment by focusing on sensations within the body. As you become mindfully aware of what you are feeling in the present moment, you can move away from automatic and reactionary responses to life and cultivate more purposeful action instead of simply defaulting to that which is habitual.

Practice just being and becoming more present and aware. Aware of the current sensations in your body. Aware of the breath moving in and out of your lungs. Know that this stillness and calm is available to you at any time and in any situation.

"When I let go of what I am, I become what I might be."
-Lao Tzu

Begin by finding a comfortable seated position away from possible distractions. Take a few slow, deep breaths through your nose. Close your eyes, and scan your body for sensations. Begin at your feet. Notice any sensations in your toes, feet and ankles. Move your awareness into your legs. Become aware of how your legs feel. Note any heaviness, tightness, discomfort, tingling or other sensations. Become aware of how your hips, buttocks and pelvis feel. Notice any sensations in these areas of your body. Relax and let go of any tension.

Bring your awareness to your stomach and lower back. Notice any tightness, discomfort, movement or other sensations. Observe the gentle rise and fall of the belly with your breath without judging it or trying to change it. Notice your chest, your upper back and shoulders. Become aware of any tension, tingling, warmth or other sensations. Note the gentle wave as your chest rises and falls with each inhale and exhale. Notice how your rib cage expands and contracts as you inhale and exhale. Observe what it feels like as the air enters and leaves your body.

Bring your awareness to your arms, wrists, hands and fingers. Notice sensations of warmth, cold, tingling, heaviness or lightness. Become aware of how the air and your clothing feel against your skin. Bring your awareness to your neck and head. Notice any tension you are holding there. As you exhale allow yourself to relax.

Let tension and stress melt away. Allow yourself to simply be present.

Become aware of sensations throughout your body of warmth, tingling, tightness and calm. As you bring your awareness to each part of your body, note whatever sensations are there. Notice any warmth and coolness, tightness or relaxation, sharp feelings or tingling. Do not try to push away these sensations, label them or judge them as good or bad. Simply notice that they are there. Allow yourself to feel whatever is occurring in the present moment without resisting. Be an objective observer.

As you scan your body for sensations, ask yourself:

- Where in my body do I feel uncomfortable sensations?
- Where in my body do I feel pleasant sensations?
- How am I experiencing negative thoughts, feelings and emotions in my body?
- How am I experiencing positive thoughts, feelings and emotions in my body?
- What makes these experiences uncomfortable?
- What makes these experiences pleasant, calming or refreshing?
- What memory or association do I feel in association with these sensations? Am I feeling and holding onto an emotional experience in my body?
- What is unbalanced in my experience, physically, emotionally or spiritually, to which my body is reacting?
- Am I resisting any of these sensations? Why?
- How can I release my resistance to what I am experiencing and allow these sensations to simply be present? How can I allow this experience to flow though?
- What can I learn from embracing and befriending these sensations and their wisdom?

Once you have observed what is uncomfortable in your body and noted the quality and experience of these sensations, begin to shift your focus to the positive in your life. Reflect on that which you feel grateful for or things which you are looking forward to in your life. Allow your heart to fill with excitement, love and gratitude.

As you feel this positivity washing over you and become relaxed and positive, you can start to expand your awareness. Listen to any sounds in your environment, and slowly open your eyes. Move forward, and enjoy the flow of your day.

As you become more focused in the present, you may notice that as you let go of resisting what is there in the moment, things begin to change and flow more easily. Ironically, our resistance to feeling and acknowledging negativity is often what allows uncomfortable sensations, thoughts and feelings to become stuck in our minds and bodies. By releasing judgment and resistance to such sensations and instead focusing on what is occurring in the present moment, you can release the negative and uncomfortable sensations and allow things to flow.

This practice allows you to break open the dam which is keeping you stuck in negativity and release the flow of the river so that it can move freely and naturally again. Notice how centered and still you feel after this exercise. Carry this stillness with you as you allow your life to flow with ease.

As you regularly practice cultivating more profound awareness, you will find that you can quickly bring yourself back to the present moment. You will be able to develop a renewed focus on the current state of your body and a recognition of any sensations you experiences. You can use this exercise as a quick practice when faced with an acute upset or unexpected frustration. Consistently fostering this awareness will help you more smoothly move through major distress and process negative and difficult emotions at an accelerated rate.

You can come back to your observations and insights from this exercise later and explore them further. As you recognize your patterns and responses to life's experiences, you may find that your body reacts with muscle contractions, tension, stress, hormonal imbalances or other reactions.

Recognize how you have responded to distress in the past, and affirm that you have a choice in how you interpret and respond to emotional turbulence and difficult life circumstances moving forward. Experiment with techniques for releasing reactionary patterns that are not supporting you. Dancing, drumming, singing, deep breathing or practicing meditation can all be constructive ways to process and deal with tension, emotions and stress.

You may also find it helpful to place your hand over an area of tension or stuck emotion. Bring your attention to the part of your body where you are holding the pain, and, as you exhale, release that tension. Feel the unsettled sensation leave your body as you calmly breathe and ride the wave of the breath. In other situations, it can be helpful to write out your emotions and struggles on paper and burn the notes, turning the tension to ashes which blow away with the wind.

By taking responsibility for old patterns, you are empowered to respond in new and creative ways. You no longer have to depend on others or outside circumstances. You hold the strength, insight and understanding within you.

PRESCRIPTION: LET GO OF POSSESSIONS AND CLEAN OUT

In order to create sacred space for growth and evolution, we often need to purge our lives of old possessions, ideas and habits. To make room in your life and home for what you truly want and love, you need to clear out things that are blocking energy, cluttering and filling up space.

Taking some time to clean-up your home and release unneeded possessions, habits, emotions and toxins is a great way to embrace the energy of forward movement in your life. You have to get rid of the old to make way for the new.

Many of us like "things". We tend to hold onto material possessions year after year. We save and stock up on things that we do not know what to do with anymore. Maybe you keep things because they hold precious memories, or they remind you of your loved ones or childhood. Sometimes old possessions feel safe. It can seem difficult to part with these precious possessions.

For good mental and physical health, we actually have two "houses" that need to be cleaned: our physical homes and our physical bodies. As we accumulate "stuff" in the form of outgrown clothes, magazines, rusty bicycles, tools and random keepsakes, our energy can become stagnant and stuck. Throw out some of that stuff, let go of the past and welcome the new energy of your happy, healthy future!

Take inventory of your home. Methodically go through the objects filling your home, and evaluate them with mindful eyes. Clear out the things that you no longer use, which are not consistent with the life you want to live or which are simply filling space or for show. See clearly which objects might need a new home or a different space in your life. Notice those things that seem consistent with the energy you want to welcome into your life as you move forward.

Choose to keep that which holds true meaning, brings authentic joy and inspires you. Be firm with your intention to create space for what you truly want. Allow yourself to let go, and recycle things which are no longer serving you. By letting go of these objects and offering them back into the world, you are honoring your authentic life. Moving the energy of old possessions in a dynamic way opens room for new potential and vibrancy to flow. Fill your life with those things which truly connect you to the fullness and richness of life!

CHAPTER 9: Crafting a Narrative of Positive Energy

EVERYTHING IS ENERGY. You create vibrations that can be positive or negative with your thoughts, words, actions and intentions. The things which you focus on and spend time dwelling on become energy in your life. As you choose your thoughts, you essentially choose what manifests in your life. Your thoughts, beliefs, attitudes and intentions can literally shape the world around you and your experience in it.

Our brains are immensely powerful. The healthy human brain can process 400 billion pieces of information each second, yet we only consciously recognize about 2,000 of those. Most of the information we take in is actually processed by our mind in order to filter out unnecessary things. The subconscious mind helps process memories, experiences and perceptions that result in your experience of life and contribute to your feelings and emotions. These, in turn, influence your conscious behavior, mindset and self. We interpret these complex inputs, emotions and experiences and shape our resulting thoughts and behaviors. Our brains also actively develop solutions for challenges and solve problems.

Your brain can contribute to healing and help you manifest your dreams and desires. In medicine, the placebo effect has been shown to help people recover even in the absence of medication, surgery or other interventions. It is clear that faith and beliefs can powerfully influence the body. In fact, research has demonstrated that those with a positive outlook frequently live almost twelve years longer than their pessimistic counterparts!

"We are shaped by our thoughts; we become what we think. When the mind is pure, joy flows like a shadow that never leaves."
-Buddha

In many ways, your perceptions of and reactions to what happens in your life can be even more powerful than what actually occurs. Thoughts carry immense energy and shape your reality. "What you think, you become" can be very true. Your influential brain can be your greatest ally and help you live a fulfilling and authentic life, but it can also contribute to fear, doubt and self-sabotage if you allow it to do so.

Each moment you have a choice to perceive situations, people and circumstances in your life as gifts that can support you and help you grow or obstacles that contribute to your struggle. Choose to break out of limiting beliefs and perceptions, and you can embrace your full potential. You are so much more than you allow yourself to be!

Practice Nurturing, Positive Self-Talk

Fortunately, you have a choice. Your thoughts, experiences and emotions are constantly being processed by the brain. Those that are aligned with the energy of gratitude, faith, positivity and hope create possibility and forward momentum. You can choose to look at everything that occurs as an opportunity or tool for positive energy. You can transform obstacles and adversity into opportunities and lessons.

Awareness is fundamental for recognizing your emotions and thoughts and making positive change. Consciousness involves the ability to remain present and aware in each moment. When you become mindful of your thoughts and slow down to notice your emotions, it is possible to acknowledge and care for your emotional needs in constructive and positive ways instead of engaging in destructive or self-defeating behavior. From this place of awareness, you are able to release fear, envy, worry, judgment, self-doubt and other negative energy.

"Don't wait for your feelings to change to take the action. Take the action and your feelings will change."
-Barbara Baron

Emotions can be intense and seem overwhelming at times. Sometimes it can be helpful to step back and separate ourselves from the grip of relentless anxiety, overwhelming fear or intense sorrow. Negative thinking can create a destructive cycle which is disempowering and limits your forward momentum. In fact studies show that it often takes up to seven positive thoughts to override the effects of one negative thought. This is why it is so important that we learn how to be mindful of our dominant thoughts and how they impact our behaviors and movement towards or away from our heart-centered goals.

You can be your own worst critic or your biggest cheerleader. It is a choice you make each time you speak to yourself. Speaking to yourself with a cynical, judgmental, criticizing voice fails to acknowledge and support your strengths, abilities and successes. Your mind and ego can create false stories that can hold you back. When you embrace your imperfections and mistakes with grace and self-forgiveness, you treat yourself as the precious being which you are.

Negative thoughts drain your energy and keep you from being in the present moment. If you think negative, frantic, depressing thoughts, they can eventually manifest themselves physically. It can be easy to get caught up in a cycle of negative thoughts which can lead to unhealthy behaviors and destructive habits. You may feel lonely and turn to the pint of ice cream in the freezer. Or you may get frustrated and say things which you do not mean.

Conversely, when you think positive, calm, encouraging thoughts, they can help you manifest what you want in life. Focus on the positive, and see how your mindset shifts. If you find yourself dwelling in the negative or focusing on problems in your life, make a conscious effort to recognize some positive blessings you are also experiencing.

You can choose to focus on gratitude, love, kindness and positivity towards yourself and others. Practice listening to and accepting compliments and concentrating on your authentic purpose. Get in touch with what you would do differently if you knew you would not be judged. Affirm that you are strong enough, good enough and valuable enough just as you are. Celebrate and utilize your strengths to make a positive impact in the world, and they will grow. Find that which truly excites you about life, and emphasize it more often. Embrace the opportunity to be your best and most authentic self!

Crafting Your Affirmative Narrative

The stories you tell yourself about your life create your personal narrative. Each day you weave this narrative with your thoughts and self-talk. Perhaps your story currently includes thoughts like "I need to lose weight," "I hate my job," "I love my husband," "I can never make enough money," "I will never be good enough," "I have gorgeous eyes" or "I love living in this city!"

Sometimes these thoughts are fleeting, but at other times they can become mantras over which we obsess. Our minds can become chaotic and distracted when they are filled with endless streams of judgments, expectations, worries, resentments and stories about what should or should not occur.

Thoughts can compound, grow and explode into something much, much larger as you place attention on them. Your personal narrative can take on an energy and life of its own. An event or stress-induced moment can trigger a thought that can quickly escalate into a narrative.

For example, your sister borrows your favorite sweater without asking, and you blow-up at her and think "I hate my family!" As the week goes on, you think negative thoughts over and over like "I have no support from my family," "I am so alone in life," and "People are always taking advantage of me." You start complaining to your mother about your sister's behavior and gossiping with your friends about how your life is not fair. Every time you interact with your sister, your narrative comes flooding back over you, even when she is being kind, respectful and supportive.

This cycle only reinforces all those negative thoughts and feelings. Before you know it, your relationship with your sister is strained, and you are fixated on the lack of support you perceive in so many areas of your life. You do not just feel a lack of support from your sister, you feel like your husband never listens, your boss is out to get you and your friends have their own agenda and are never there for you.

It can be difficult to choose to construct a positive narrative in a negative, complaining world. There is a ton of toxicity around us, and it can be easy to get drawn in. Gossip, frenemies, reality TV, online forums and magazines can seem filled with venting, struggle, judgment and negativity.

On the other hand, you have the power to create positive narratives as well. Choosing to be content and have a positive outlook can turn a stressful situation into a learning opportunity and change your circumstances for the better. When you choose a positive interpretation of your life circumstances, it can make everything more enjoyable. Life will flow more easily.

"We can complain because rose bushes have thorns, or rejoice because thorn bushes have roses."
-Abraham Lincoln

Creating a positive narrative is not about being naïve, in denial or blinded to life. Expressing true emotions such as anxiety, sadness, disappointment or unease is not necessarily being negative. In fact it can be healthy to express your true emotions, even when they are difficult, in positive ways and forms. Difficult emotions are a normal part of the human experience and can be a part of a constructive narrative. When you are honest and vulnerable in your authentic story, you can acknowledge negative emotions and hardships while remaining optimistic, kind, hopeful and forgiving.

The key is how you react and move forward when you are faced with a challenging situation. You can cultivate an awareness and mindfulness that allows you to escape the stories that the mind creates about the past and the future. What endures when you find stillness, quiet the mind and open the heart, is a genuine truth away from the chaos and constant shifting of the superficial world.

When you lose your job do you say to yourself "You are such a failure, you will never be able to support yourself. Look at you and your life. You are a mess." Or do you look at the situation and conclude, "This will be a struggle for a while, but it is a great opportunity for me to finally take that leap into the career I have been dreaming about. I can face my fears and do this."

Choosing to look at your situation from an optimistic and hopeful stance instead of being mean, hurtful and toxic creates a realistic narrative that acknowledges the ups and downs in life. This approach applies to many aspects of life—career, relationships, family, health, personal growth and spirituality.

Do not deprive yourself and the world of all that you have to offer. Dream big, and own your authentic truth. As you fulfill your passionate purpose in the world, you proclaim your truth not in loud words but with meaningful action. As you reinforce your inner spirit, you authentically express your greatness in the world.

Place your faith in yourself and something greater. Remain true to the best that is within you. This will allow you to connect more deeply and meaningfully with others and tap into the natural and peaceful flow of life. Open up your heart and allow your inner light to shine!

"Dwell on the beauty of life. Watch the stars, and see yourself running with them."
-Marcus Aurelius

PRESCRIPTION: REFRAME YOUR GOALS AND RETRAIN YOUR BRAIN

Your subconscious cannot distinguish between visualizing the future, dwelling in the past and existing in the reality of the present. You have the power to imagine a positive outcome and embed these thoughts deep in your brain. As you make a conscious choice to focus on the positive, you retrain your brain and create energy that reflects these positive statements. This attracts more positive experiences and situations into your life!

Think about a goal that you have had for a while but have not yet been able to fulfill for whatever reason. Reflect on all the reasons that have held you back from achieving this goal. List all the stories you tell yourself about why you cannot easily move forward or overcome a specific issue or challenge.

- What beliefs, thought patterns, things and situations stand between you and your goal?
- What has kept you stuck? Why are you not moving forward?
- Where are you suffering?

Look at the list you have made. Turn each negative belief and limiting thought into a positive affirmation. Come up with positive statements for each negative thought. Use the present tense as if you have already overcome these challenges. Focus on how you want to feel, think and be. Place yourself into the state of mind you want to achieve.

Take these positive statements and repeat them often. Sit quietly several times a day and repeat your positive reframes. Even if you only take a few moments to do this, you will start to notice amazing changes over time. Be patient, and give your brain time to absorb the new perspective. Trust that it is working.

Consider how you can move forward. List those things that speak to your soul even if they seem outrageous.

- What is something that you could do to take massive, meaningful action?
- What are sensible, logical steps you could take to get yourself unstuck?

You are the creator and designer of your life! With trust, faith and dedication, you will transform your life. Reprogramming your brain by consciously reflecting on positive thoughts empowers you to redirect your energy. Take back your power to exude positive energy into the world. As you focus on the vast possibilities along your path, your life can change in amazing ways.

PRESCRIPTION: LOOK FOR THE GOOD AND BE GENTLE WITH YOURSELF

This week take ten to fifteen minutes each day to reflect and journal on the following questions. Use this time and practice to train your mind to seek out the positive in the world around you and to focus on the good in your everyday experiences. As you begin to more mindfully recognize positive experiences and emotions in your life, become aware of what it feels like in your mind, body and soul to enjoy such pleasurable and uplifting experiences. Sense and feel these pleasant occurrences permeating your being and becoming your reality. Remember and reflect on the good.

- What positive events occurred today? How did you experience joy in this day?
- What made you feel good today? What experiences did you have that filled you with a sense of joy and fulfillment?

Cultivating a positive mindset supports the manifestation of your authentic passionate purpose and helps you bring about that which you wish to create in your life. Commit to being truly authentic. Remain gentle and compassionate with yourself. You are more likely to successfully reach your goals when you approach them with self-compassion, patience and non-judgment. When looking at your intentions and goals for your life, focus on acknowledging your strength and progress. Honor the fact that you are exactly where you are meant to be right now when you are living in alignment with your passionate purpose.

To keep moving forward with your goals, it is important to treat yourself with respect. Be gentle with yourself, and acknowledge your forward movement instead of getting stuck on what you have not yet achieved or areas where you feel overwhelmed or unsure. When you notice the negative voice popping up in your head, hit the pause button and ask yourself a few key questions.

- Examine what your mind is telling you. Consider if this message is actually true. Are you creating stories that are helpful and supportive of your intentions?
- Look at what you are telling yourself, and consider if it is inspiring you to move towards your authentic purpose. Is it necessary and supportive of your big dreams?

Explore these questions with compassion. Keep an open mind and nonjudgmental attitude. Affirm the possibilities which can manifest when you get out of your own way and love and support yourself. Remain conscious of the power of your thoughts. Acknowledge their power, and use them to your advantage to create positive patterns. Embrace your emerging potential, and spread positive energy out into the world!

PRESCRIPTION: IDENTIFY YOUR THOUGHT PATTERNS

Find a quiet space and sit comfortably. Take a few deep breaths to center yourself and relax. Reflect and journal on the following ideas concerning your thought patterns. Use this time to gain insight into the powerful impact which your thoughts and self-talk have on your visions, aspirations and life.

Think about the thoughts that seem to pop up repeatedly in your mind.

- What thoughts do you have about yourself, your dreams, your goals and your life that habitually enter your self-talk?

- What are your dominant thoughts about yourself?
- What repeated thought patterns do you have about your dreams and goals?
- What habitual thoughts do you have about your life?

For each of the thought patterns you identified above, consider how those beliefs move you toward or away from your heart-centered goals Look at how your thought patterns and self-talk are impacting your life.

- Are you willing to change negative and fear-based self-talk into positive self-talk?
- What are you willing to do to transform habitual belief patterns that are moving you away from your dreams and goals into thought patterns that reinforce and support your authentic life?

PRESCRIPTION: DISCOVER THE POWER OF PAUSE

Realize that you can press pause in any moment. You have the choice to recognize the stream of thoughts running through your mind in any instant and to elect to step back from the momentum of invalid, irrational, destructive habits and thought patterns.

Choose to step outside the pain of being stuck in old anger that holds you back. Opt to overcome the constriction and limitation imposed on you by your constraining thoughts. Decide to let go of the chaos that takes over when you allow your feelings to rule your thoughts and life. Open your eyes to your core power to live in a way that is aligned, authentic, intelligent and affirming of your deepest desires. You will find that clarity arises as you overcome the overwhelm.

As you pause, recognize your current patterns, and then ask yourself the following questions.

- In this present moment, what do I really want to feel?
- How do I want to choose to react?
- What energy do I want to bring into my life?

The answers to these questions will lead you to your true intentions, desires and passions. You can find authentic happiness and a peace and clarity that will bring freedom to your life.

As you pause your thoughts, notice the beliefs and feelings that grab your attention.

- What is getting in the way of your joy, peace and happiness?
- Are you stuck in a narrative of anger, inadequacy, unease or fear?
- Do you repeatedly perceive yourself as a victim of your past and circumstances?
- Do you define yourself by your suffering?

Realize that these stressful stories are present but do not have control over you. You can choose to let them go without playing into them or acting on them.

In the space you create when you pause, step back and separate yourself from your habitual stories, you discover the freedom and ease that exists as you step out of your own way. In this stillness, there is potential for you to embrace your whole, calm, relaxed self. This is the place where you can be in touch with your inner wisdom, make wise decisions that come from love instead of fear and overcome previously self-imposed limitations.

By pausing and recognizing your thoughts and emotions, you realize how false definitions and stories constrain your true potential. You create space and possibilities for forward growth. You have the power to choose to live fully in the present and to overcome any self-imposed boundaries. Open your heart, and clear your mind. Here you will find an effortless freedom that leads you to genuine peace in each moment.

PRESCRIPTION: DEVELOP A MORE POSITIVE PERSONAL NARRATIVE

What thoughts do you have about your life? Are you creating an ongoing dialogue with yourself that reinforces your talents, encourages growth and supports your positive evolution, or are you harping on the past, berating yourself, criticizing others and blaming your circumstances? Where did these thoughts and stories come from? How are they influenced by others—your family, coworkers, friends, the media—in positive and/or negative ways?

There are several strategies you can adopt to reinforce and create a more positive personal narrative in your life.

Identify Sources of Negativity: Consider the inputs, energies and words you take in each day. Contemplate how the people that you speak with, the television you watch, the articles that you read, the music that you listen to, the groups you engage in and the conversations you participate in influence your personal narrative about your life. Negativity cultivates negativity, so engaging with too many negative people can reinforce an outlook of cynicism, destruction and pessimism.

Consider how you can cut out toxicity and find positively-focused inputs in your life. Consider unsubscribing from that snarky magazine, logging off of your social media that is filled with complaining friends, cutting off a draining relationship and turning off the critical television show. The first step in crafting your positive personal narrative is to remove the stream of constant negative inputs, even those that seem unrelated to your personal thoughts and situation.

Seek Out Sources of Positivity: Replace those negative inputs with positive ones. Fill your social media feed with positive images and encouraging friends. Watch a documentary that inspires personal growth. Spend time with friends that support you and are enthusiastic in their own pursuits. As you surround yourself with more positivity, you will become more positive yourself. Even if you do not fully feel it yet, open yourself up to outside sources of positivity, and allow that small spark to take hold.

Challenge Your Negative Self-Talk: In order to stop negative thinking in its tracks and cease to let it snowball into a negative personal narrative for your life, you need to consistently identify and replace negative thoughts and self-talk. It is important to reinforce positive energy in your life by choosing to remain realistic yet optimistic in your self-narrative.

It is not about living in denial or sugar-coating everything. Instead, you can reframe your negative thoughts by choosing to focus on the positive potential or aspects of the situation. You can shift your view of the outcome to be more forgiving and realistic. For example, if you are struggling to make healthier choices, you can reframe your self-criticism with something like "I choose to eat that chocolate cake today, but I can also choose to have a healthy dinner and allow room for balance in my life." or "I had to take the kids to baseball practice today, so I missed my gym time and I feel guilty, but life is a balancing act. I am so lucky to have a full, happy life with my family and children. It's normal that I feel overwhelmed and frustrated in this moment, but this feeling won't last."

CHAPTER 10: Find the Courage to Shift into Compassion and Forgiveness

LIVING YOUR LIFE FROM a place of unconditional love, for yourself and others, is another key element of *The Whole Cure*. When you act from love, with kindness and compassion, you can add a magical ease and grace to your life. As you approach life without judgment towards yourself or others, you will notice that there is a shift in your perception and experience of life. Compassion enhances our connections with ourselves, with those we interact with and with the world around us.

Often we approach life from a place of fear and self-doubt. Fear can lead you to hold onto assumptions that do not serve you. You may find that you cannot let go of grudges, have difficulty forgiving and feel insecure. Fortunately, when you are able to let go of this insecurity and release the fear of scarcity, you can live with gratitude and an acceptance of the abundance of life. Consciously cultivating an attitude of compassion, forgiveness and kindness allows you to live a life in the spirit of loving abundance.

"The amount of happiness that you have depends on the amount of freedom you have in your heart."
-Thich Nhat Hanh

Courageously Cultivate Compassion

Compassion is a sense of understanding and appreciation for the pain and experiences of others. While it may not always be easy to comprehend the suffering around us, a compassionate heart strives to forgive, to reduce anguish and to embrace kind action. Pain is real, and suffering is a frequent part of life. Yet when you reach out, connect with others and open up your heart with thoughtful forgiveness, love and empathy, you tap into the healing power of compassion and true connection.

To practice greater compassion, it is important to start with yourself. Begin by opening up your awareness to the stress, fear, doubt, anger, disappointment and frustration that you face in your daily life. Accept these sensations with an open awareness instead of trying to suppress them or run away from them.

Examine the causes of your suffering. Are you holding onto an idea of how your life should be? How you think you should act? What you feel you must accomplish? Often the cause of your suffering arises from an ideal you create in your mind. As you reconnect with your authentic self and cultivate your passionate purpose, you can begin to let go of the construct of who you thought you were supposed to be and embrace the amazing spirit you truly are!

It is important to reconnect with the truth that you are infinitely loveable. Love is our innate essence and fundamental nature. When we are unkind to ourselves or others, we are not aligned with who we truly are.

Opening yourself up to this vulnerability brings a new realm of possibilities as you share your authentic self with the world without shame, regret or doubt. This is turn allows an unconditional love, acceptance and compassion to flow into your life. This freedom brings a deeper sense of forgiveness, sincerity and unrestricted love for yourself that translates into a level of genuine compassion for others as well.

As you cultivate self-compassion, you can apply that kindness on a larger scale as well. Realizing that negative experiences, judgment and offense do not stem from any personal lack, character flaws or insecurities allows you to shift your negative self-talk. As you are able to embrace yourself with self-love, forgiveness, acceptance and compassion, you awaken a place of infinite love that changes the way you perceive of the outside world as well.

Remember that we are all interconnected. As humans, we share common fears, doubts, uncertainties and frustrations. You are not alone in your suffering, confusion and difficulty. Unconditional, pure love sees only that which unites us as one.

"The whole idea of compassion is based on a keen awareness of the interdependence of all these living beings."
-Thomas Merton

When you focus on the positive in others and seek out expressions of love in the world around you, cultivating compassion will come with greater ease. Everyone has something positive in their complex nature. With this perspective, you can more easily find a stance of understanding, meaning and love.

Cultivating compassion means acting from a balanced perspective. It does not require you to sacrifice your own needs for those of others. Instead, it involves acting from a place which recognizes what is truly in the highest interest of the whole. From this perspective, compassion can be limitless. It does not run out.

Choose To Live From Love Rather Than Fear
"The heart has eyes which the brain knows nothing of."
-Charles H. Perkhurst

Instead of reacting to less than ideal circumstances, negative comments or destructive insults from others with personal offense, you can cultivate an awareness that these situations are not personal reflections of your inner worth. This perspective allows you to shift your fear-based reactions into ones based in love. You start to be able to see the other in you and you in the other. When you live from a place of self-love and project compassion out into the world, that humanity is reflected back to you.

One way to cultivate greater compassion, love and kindness is through the acknowledgement of that which is positive and loving in your life. As you recognize the blessings that already exist in your life, you activate the energy of love. Focusing on gratitude ignites a sense of compassion and connection with those around you.

As you concentrate on seeing your connections with others, compassion will naturally flow. It will not require effort or striving but instead will become a part of natural existence. Focusing energy on love, patience, empathy, appreciation and that which is good in the world allows the experience of compassion to permeate your life and drowns out resentment, anger, hatred, fear and judgment.

This compassion connects you with the common human experience and helps you relate to others with greater openness and empathy. This enhanced sense of connection, enriches an appreciation of unity and minimizes perception of differences. Compassion flows when you recognize that, despite distinctive beliefs, values and experiences, we are united souls seeking understanding and love in life.

"Kindness in words creates confidence. Kindness in thinking creates profoundness. Kindness in giving creates love."
-Lao Tzu

You can ease the suffering you observe around you as well as that which arises in your heart by cultivating open, loving and non-judgmental connections. This can be as simple as sharing a smile with a stranger on the subway or opening your heart to accepting a loved one for the person she truly is.

Let go of expectations of that person, and permit yourself to connect at a deeper soul level. Allow yourself to embrace the compassionate connection with each soul you come into contact with in your life.

Actions evolving from love create more joy, happiness and abundance in your life!

Forgiveness

"The weak can never forgive. Forgiveness is the attribute of the strong."
-Mahatma Gandhi

Forgiveness employs the transforming power of love. Unfortunately, we all experience hurt, pain and trauma in our lives. When the pain and hurt, whether intentional or unintentional, are intense enough, you may hold onto anger, depression, offense, guilt and resentment. This cycle of pain can deepen and intensify as you hold onto the memory of the transgression and play it over and over in your mind. This cycle can become consuming and damaging, as you become filled with resentment and block love from emerging.

If you are able to recognize that you hold onto offenses and perceived slights out of hurt, fear and pain, you can begin to let go and forgive. What does it cost you to hold onto past grievances?

Forgiveness is not about blindly accepting that what happened in the past is necessarily okay or can be forgotten. Instead, it is about acknowledging what has occurred, accepting the consequences and taking back your power by no longer allowing that situation to drain your energy.

When you forgive yourself or others, you choose to look at a situation differently. You make a choice on a deeper level to see a situation though a lens of compassion, understanding and wisdom which is rooted in compassion. Accepting the past, even when it is painful, can open up the possibility of renewal, openness, freedom and love. Practicing forgiveness reduces anger, depression, stress, hurt and fear. From this perspective, you are able to embrace compassion and cultivate greater hope, peace, confidence and healing.

Forgiveness is a choice. It is a powerful stance that can transform lives. Although it may feel safer to hold onto memories, trauma and thoughts of the past, this inability to move beyond bygone hurts can keep you stuck in the past. Forgiveness requires that you accept where you are in the present moment and gives you the freedom to stop judging from a negative, fear-based energy. When you are able to truly forgive, you can break free of the past and become liberated.

Freely expressing compassion lays the groundwork for forgiving yourself and others. When you can begin to express loving forgiveness to yourself and others, you can focus on moving forward. Taking a stance of love and compassion allows you to cleanse past pain and let go of hurt feelings. In this place, compassion can begin to grow.

PRESCRIPTION: ACT OUT OF LOVE

Make a conscious effort this week to pause throughout your day and look at the world with an open heart. As you approach a relationship, confrontation or situation, pause and take a few deep breaths. Allow your tension to soften and any anger or fear to melt away. Instead of reacting to fear or uncertainty with constriction and a closed off heart, soften your heart and choose to approach the world in an open and accepting manner.

Whenever you are faced with a challenging interaction or a difficult decision, take a moment to examine the intention behind your actions.

- Are you trying to hold onto control?
- Are you reacting from a place of fear?
- Are you attempting to grasp at a possession, a person or time itself?

As you look at your motivation, make a conscious choice to step into a place of love, kindness and compassion. Can you change how you relate from a fear-based to a love-based stance? Begin to cultivate an openness and acceptance of the world around you, yourself and others.

Taking action out of love means that you act directly, openly, honestly and from a place of generosity of spirit and heart! Pause in your day and think about if you are acting out of fear or from a place of love. When you act out of love you attract positive people, emotions and experiences into your life. Conversely, acting out of fear attracts that which you fear. When you choose to act from love, notice how it changes your relationships and your experience of life.

Before you do anything in your life, ask yourself "Am I doing this out of love?" Before you decide how to speak to yourself or others, how to nourish yourself or what actions to take, take a moment to reflect on whether you are acting as an expression of love? Allow yourself to remain open and truthful. When you feel love within you, act on that. Speak, act and express yourself from your heart.

Examine how you express love with your thoughts and actions towards yourself and others. Acting out of love helps you face the world in an open and accepting way. It helps you remain receptive to love instead of constricting and closing off your heart. As you complete this prescription, think about ways in which you can open your heart more fully and deeply. Notice the shift this creates in your relationships, experiences and energy.

PRESCRIPTION: LOVE YOURSELF FIRST

Compassion starts with yourself. As you are able to open your heart and accept yourself unconditionally, you can begin to cultivate enhanced compassion and empathy for others as well.

Find a quiet space and sit comfortably. Take a few deep breaths to center yourself and relax. Reflect and journal on the following ideas concerning your thought patterns and how they impact your goals, relationships, energy, dreams and life experiences.

Go within and connect with yourself. Think about something you are struggling to accept about yourself. Perhaps you need to forgive yourself for something or you would like to become more open and accepting of your authentic self.

Imagine the compassion that you want to feel towards others, and first direct that love, forgiveness and acceptance towards yourself. Express empathy for your own struggles. Open your heart to accepting all the parts of yourself, even those which you are ashamed of or would rather change.

Hold a conversation with your inner critic. As you open your heart and express compassion towards yourself, notice any objections that arise from your inner critic. Write down the criticisms, disapprovals, comments and accusations that your negative inner voice proclaims.

Address each statement with a rebuttal from a place of compassion, unconditional love and self-acceptance. Stick up for yourself as you would for a dear friend. Write down a compassionate response to each self-criticism. For example, "I am only human, I do not need to be perfect."

Speak to yourself as you would to a loved one, without criticism, judgment or reproach. Remain gentle with yourself. Accept what is and has been. Acknowledge where you are now, and have faith in where you will go.

"Your task is not to seek for love, but merely to seek and find all the barriers within yourself you have built against it."
-Rumi

Use this exercise as a chance to liberate yourself from the pain of past experiences, break free of self-imposed limitations and challenge negative beliefs. Release the pattern of labeling yourself, your experiences and your behaviors. You are so much more than a label. Allow yourself to be comfortable with your authentic self without outside expectations.

Express compassion for your inner soul-driven self. Recognize her talents, worth and immense abilities. Know that you have the tools you need to overcome your inner critic and practice self-compassion. As negative emotions and self-criticisms arise, acknowledge them and let them go. This ability to break free of old patterns and fears will give you the freedom and energy to embrace your passionate purpose and live a life that resonates with your true path.

Realize that challenges like stress, anger, fear, doubt and frustration are normal emotions that do not need to limit you. Embrace the challenges you face and acknowledge your inner strength and ability to move through and beyond them. Practice self-growth rather than trying to "fix" something. Focus on strengthening what is right and working for you while building up your inner capacity for love and acceptance.

Ultimately, you need to embrace yourself as you are now in this moment with a loving and open heart. This allows you to let go, trust and place your faith in yourself and your ability to be strong, resilient and capable of coping with life.

From this place, you will be free to live with love, compassion and empathy. You will be able to relax and let go of controlling your past, your feelings and other people's perceptions and reactions. Letting go and forgiving gives you the freedom to simply be.

PRESCRIPTION: RELATE FROM COMPASSION

Think about the relationships in your life. Are there any situations in which you react with fear? Take an inventory of the people you interact with regularly and identify any relationships in which you are afraid, aggravated, apprehensive or unsettled. Perhaps your boss consistently puts you down? Maybe your sister is always belittling you? Does it seem like your father always berates you and disapproves of all of your life choices? Do you have a friend who you have disappointed repeatedly?

Think about these situations and the circumstances that lead to these patterns of interaction. How do you feel when you are with each person? Have you developed a pattern of reacting in order to protect yourself or deal with the fear, hurt or disappointment? How does this stance serve you currently? What would you like to do, say or feel differently?

In your mind, imagine visiting with each of these individuals. Practice approaching each situation from a place of courageous love. See yourself approaching that relationship with an open heart. Cultivate the courage to forgive and act from a stance of compassion. How does it feel when you adopt an attitude that you will simply bless this person, forgive them and express gratitude and kindness into the universe? Notice if your fear diminishes.

If it feels appropriate, cultivate this stance in your real life interactions with each person as well. You can try ending each interaction with this individual with a moment of open stillness where the two of you can express your appreciations, apprehensions and regrets. Allow for a chance to acknowledge the kindness of the other or express your concerns, qualms or outlook. Notice if the quality of your encounters begins to shift with this openness.

Note the different vibrational energy that you bring to the relationships and interactions. Observe any shifts you feel and how your relationships and interactions evolve when you adopt a courageous and compassionate mindset and step out of your fears.

PRESCRIPTION: EMBRACING COMPASSION AND EXPRESSING LOVE

When your heart connects with another, love flows. Your full, loving heart gives of itself naturally as you feel compassion. Allowing love to flow without restriction, opens up your heart and taps into the depth of transformative and healing pure love that unites us as one humanity.

Find a place to sit quietly without interruptions. Sit or lie down comfortably and close your eyes. Bring your attention to your breath for a few moments. Notice the gentle flow of the breath in and out. Allow your belly to fill and empty as it rises and falls with each inhale and exhale.

Remember a recent time when you truly felt happy. Connect with this feeling of joy. Perhaps you spent time with a beloved friend or walked through the forest with the sound of the wind in the leaves and the birds chirping above.

Envision this joy as a bright, glowing, white light. Feel it wash over you. Allow that feeling of pure joy to spread throughout your body, from head to toe. Feel the warmth, love, care, bliss, concern, togetherness and peace within you. Spread these emotions of joy, love and compassion through and around you. Feel the love pervading every space of your being and encircling you. Allow yourself to rest peacefully in this blissful love.

Next, envision someone you love dearly. Gather some of the joy and compassion which is in and around you. Give this kindness as a gift to your beloved. Allow him or her to have all the joy and love you feel bubbling up in your heart. Notice that as you spread this compassion and love to the other person, you still have an endless bountiful source of love within you as well. Even as you give of your compassion to your loved one, the sense of joy and love within you in not diminished. You are including the other within these feelings, allowing both your and their happiness to grow.

Now, envision someone you need to forgive. Perhaps there is someone who has mistreated you or caused suffering. Instead of reacting towards this person with anger, mistrust or alienation, remain calm and reflective. Gather some of the immense joy and compassion which is in and around you. Quiet your mind and focus your attention on your heart. Try to imagine the suffering that person must have been experiencing for him or her to have mistreated you.

Allow the joy around you to melt away any negative emotions in your heart. Feel your negative feelings being diffused by this joy and transformed into compassion and understanding. Tap into a place of compassion and forgiveness within you. Express kindness as a gift to this person who has hurt you. Allow him or her to share in the joy and love you feel bubbling up in your heart. Imagine sending love, compassion and forgiveness to him or her. Notice how, as you spread this compassion and love to the other person, you still have an endless bountiful source of love within you as well. Even as you give of your compassion and open to forgiveness, the sense of joy and love within you is not diminished.

Reflect on what it is like to allow yourself to experience this sense of endless joy. Where do you believe this feeling of happiness comes from? From what place are you able to access compassion and forgiveness? Journal about your thoughts and feelings. Reflect on what this experience is like for you and how it applies to your relationships and life.

PRESCRIPTION: STEP INTO LOVE

In the heat of the moment, when you are frustrated, scared, angry or hurt, it is easy to use words that you might not really mean. When you get defensive or act out of fear, you may find that you express yourself in a way that disrespects others and is not true to your deeper intentions. You may reflect back on these moments and interactions and wish you had handled things differently. In these times, you may notice that the natural current of love has stopped flowing freely.

Fortunately, you can begin to retrain your heart, mind and body to react and live in a more empowering and loving way. You can choose to step into a place of love. From this stance, you will find your relationships become more genuine and fulfilling. Your interactions flow with greater ease and you feel confident that you are doing the right thing.

As you work on this prescription, become more aware of how you interact with others and what it feels like after these exchanges. Notice any instances when you jump to respond before really connecting with your heart. Instead of reacting immediately, take a moment to pause, remain quiet and pay attention. Truly listen to the other person and what he or she is expressing as well as the emotions, thoughts and sensations that arise within you.

As you find a moment of stillness, bring your attention to your breath. Breathe slowly and deeply. Often when we become scared, angry, frustrated or hurt we breathe shallowly and rapidly or completely hold our breath. This only adds to the physiological turmoil. Instead, remain mindful of your breath. Breathe in slowly through your nose and out slowly through your mouth. Allow the breath to bring you a sense of calm. As you reset your nervous system, ease stress and refocus, you will be able to think more clearly and connect with a place of love and compassion.

Release situations which you cannot control and people who are stuck in a place of negativity. Know that others' behaviors and reactions are not about you. You have a choice about how you react. It is up to you to choose the type of energy you take on and put out into the world.

When faced with an interaction, bring your attention to your heart. Acknowledge any sensations and emotions that arise within you. Recognize any stressful or negative qualities. As you breathe deeply and slowly, bring in compassion and love with each breath. Allow this cleansing, positive energy to support you and fill you with kindness, caring and support. Generate a growing compassion within yourself as you inhale deeply. As this love begins to flow, feel this loving energy flowing around and out from you as you exhale. Send compassion to the other person as you exhale fully.

As you breathe and feel grounded and centered, expand your awareness to all living beings. Feel this soothing, supportive and loving kindness flow into you and out to all beings. When you are ready, allow yourself to gently rest in the tender compassion of this glowing, loving light for a few moments.

Allow love to flow. Move forward from a place of kindness and compassion. Forgive when it is appropriate and necessary. Move on when that is needed. Take care of yourself. Remember that you can tap into and expand this compassionate loving kindness at any time and place.

Notice how this enhanced awareness that you bring to your interactions changes the energy you experience. Compassionate connections reduce stress, heighten support and allow us to flourish as a community. Love grants you an inner freedom in your mind and relationships. It frees you from the control of negative emotions. You have the capacity to step into love!

CHAPTER 11: Conquer Fear and Overwhelm to Live Mindfully in the Present Moment

Fear can be a powerful emotion. It can take over our thoughts and paralyze our lives if we allow it to do so. Life can be full of "what ifs"—what if my plans do not work out, what if I do not succeed, what if I made the wrong choice, what if I cannot cope, what if he does not like me, what if I am not good enough. These limiting thoughts can be endless.

How much of your time do you spend in your head worrying about the future and reprocessing the past? It is easy to allow your mind to become flooded with anxious thoughts, preoccupied with perceptions of the past and consumed with worries about the future. When you focus on your fears, you may become paralyzed and afraid of making the wrong choice.

"The secret of health for both mind and body is not to mourn for the past, worry about the future, but to live in the present moment wisely and earnestly."
-Buddha

Fear arises out of insecurity and creates thoughts that can lead to actions which are not aligned with your true purpose. Similarly, worry is rarely productive as you fixate on uncertainty and an amorphous future threat. You may experience excessive worry, high levels of anxiety, obsessive thoughts, compulsive behaviors, anger, bitterness, greed, depression, sadness and self-doubt. If you regularly allow your thoughts to be preoccupied with the past and consumed with future worries, it is easy to become stuck and overwhelmed.

Fear and worry also negatively impact our bodies, especially our immune systems. Fear-based thoughts increase the levels of stress hormones like cortisol in our bodies. This impairs the coordination and function of the immune system. Anxiety can also squelch your enthusiasm, drown out your passions, close off opportunities, inhibit you from moving outside of your comfort zone and impede you from moving forward.

When you acknowledge fear without giving it power, you can move forward with courage and overcome obstacles. Rather than be consumed by worry, choose to be curious and open to possibilities. Resolve to consider barriers, challenges and obstacles as opportunities for growth rather than potential catastrophizes. Instead of dreading these situations and fixating on all the things that could go wrong, acknowledge your fears and choose to not feed into them. Recognize that your fears are there to try to protect you, and allow yourself to let go of them as you recognize that you do not need them to keep you stuck.

"Our deepest fear is not that we are inadequate. Our deepest fear is that we are powerful beyond measure."
-Marianne Williamson

Acknowledge and Reframe Your Fears

Fear, stress and worry come from your perception of your life. Stress is not a direct consequence of the circumstances you experience but instead results from the meaning you assign to such events.

In many situations, stress arises when we are afraid of making mistakes, causing disappointment, harming someone, being judged or letting someone down. We fear rejection, getting our hearts broken, betrayal, loss of power, discomfort or not having or being enough.

You know fear is infiltrating your mind when you have thoughts of negativity, self-doubt, judgment, anxiety, self-criticism, hopelessness and unease. These fear-based emotions can keep you from moving forward when you give them power and allow them to keep you stuck.

Fortunately, you can choose to objectively assess stressors, acknowledge them and reframe your response to them. You can adopt an attitude of strength rather than overwhelm. By acknowledging fears, calming worry and reframing your response from one based in perceived stress to one that is based in composed truth, you free your mind from the unnecessary suffering caused by anticipation.

Thoughts that are aligned with an energy of trust, gratitude, faith and positivity allow for expansion and envisioning of what is possible. It is your assessment of a situation and the emotional response to that perception which determine the impact the experience has on your body, mind and emotions. When you stay present, you can more easily relax the body, focus the mind and remain grounded in the stillness of the present.

It is important to have a clear understanding of what is holding you back in order to constructively address it. How do you react to triggers of stress and overwhelm? If you notice tension building and your thoughts spiraling out of control, pause and find stillness in the present.

As you acknowledge the outcomes which you are most afraid of, you can identify what you *do* want to happen. Fearful thoughts often point you towards those things which you need to address in order to grow personally, emotionally and spiritually. Fear can serve as a mirror showing you where you need to pay attention. Focusing on the positive outcomes you desire helps you to determine the steps you need to take to reach those results.

Planning for success and positive outcomes begins when you decide what you actually desire. As you focus on the end result, your subconscious will automatically direct you toward that positive outcome. You will open yourself up to seeking constructive solutions for challenges, tackling problems and achieving your goals and dreams. Having a positive outlook and staying focused on a clear vision of success allows you to access new ideas, opportunities, creativity and talents that support you in achieving your goals.

This approach allows you to transform old, destructive patterns of fear and worry into expansive, joyful, passionate experiences of your true self. As you activate the energy of your passionate purpose, you tap into the natural flow of life and build on the intelligent, purposeful energy along your path.

Moving towards your heart-driven vision, activates safety, trust and calm that awakens your passions and fills you with a deeply-rooted peace and security. This positive energy protects and propels you forward with a recognition that changes and uncertainty will take place, but that you can calmly and competently deal with whatever happens.

Learning to Embrace Calm Certainty in an Uncertain World

As you chase a positive pursuit, you are energized by your alignment with your passionate purpose instead of being drained and suppressed by constantly struggling to avoid your fears. Acknowledging and clarifying your fears and doubts allows you to utilize them to guide you towards a path of joy and fulfillment. A fear which you have identified and verbalized has much less power over you than one that is lurking in your mind and heart.

The stronger your ability to remain grounded in the present, the greater your chances of addressing problems head on instead of becoming bogged down by what may or may not happen. Staying in the present is fundamental to avoiding excessive worry. When you cultivate mindfulness, you can focus away from hypothetical concerns that may develop in the future and instead remain in the present where you are aware of your thoughts and their consequences.

Acknowledgement of the present and acceptance of the situation help to stop the negative cycle. This approach allows you to reframe your fears to work for you as you tackle decisions in the here and now. Non-worriers are better able to test out constructive solutions to a problem and remain more flexible in the way they think about situations. By tapping into the stillness of the present moment, non-worriers can remain clear and focused without becoming sucked into a negative thinking rut.

This stability allows for a sense of perspective in which you can distance yourself from a situation and hypothetical negative outcomes. You can enhance your perspective by realistically considering the likelihood that the worst case scenario will actually occur. You can also stop the cycle of worry by getting to the root of the true situation and looking at the immediate concern. Work to identify the current issue that is happening right now instead of jumping ahead to hypothetical catastrophic outcomes. Stopping the worry cycle early on helps to keeps things in perspective and makes conquering problems more realistic and achievable.

Taking this stance helps you move from problem-generation to problem-solving. Stopping yourself from incessantly fixating on anticipating potential future problems frees up energy and attention for tackling your present goals. This expands your ability to see positive outcomes even in seemingly bleak situations. From an open-minded, calm stance in the present, you are able to see that there could be a positive outcome to a negative event. Use negative feelings to key you into what is causing those emotions and help you make informed decisions.

When you challenge your beliefs about who you are, what you are capable of and what the world has in store for you, you can break down barriers that hold you back and open up space for personal growth. Starting with overcoming even one fear creates a shift in perception and self-esteem.

As you focus on loving thoughts towards yourself and others, you express security and comfort with your true identity. When you live from a place of love instead of fear, you experience joy, forgiveness, happiness, gratitude, generosity and peace. This supports the body's functions and balances the immune system.

"People have a hard time letting go of their suffering. Out of a fear of the unknown, they prefer suffering that is familiar."
-Thich Nhat Hanh

PRESCRIPTION: STOP FEEDING THE WORRY MONSTER

A big step in escaping from the cycle of anxiety and worry is to cultivate an awareness and curiosity. Instead of allowing yourself to become consumed by worry and fixated in the past and future, choose to be curious of the thoughts which flood your mind.

When you notice anxious thoughts, pause, step back and observe them. Notice the impact these fears are having on your life and your potential for forward growth. Bring your attention to feelings, emotions and sensations in your body. Is your body locked up in fear? Are you holding tension in specific places? Notice how powerful these anxious thoughts and feelings can be.

Take some deep breaths, and shift your attention away from these anxieties and the tendency to drift into the past and project into the future. Instead simply rest with your breath in the present moment. Become aware, calm and centered. This will bring an immediate sense of relief.

As you cease to feed the worrying thoughts, the tension subsides, and you can rest with ease and calm in the present moment. This is where you will find clarity and quiet. From this calm you can make wise, centered decisions and see how they can align with your authentic purpose. In the present, you can recognize that life is unfolding just as it should and that worry and fear are optional.

Instead of needing to figure out and control everything in your life, you can begin to relax, let go and trust. As you let go and release the limitations imposed by fear, you open up a space for creativity, appreciation, wonder and ease in your life. You can step back and get out of your own way, allowing your life to flow as you stop struggling. Instead of resisting, fearing, dreading and doubting everything, you focus on what is available to you and receive what life offers.

Remember this shift of your attention whenever you notice worry or fear creeping into your day. As you quiet the noise, you will have clarity about how to move forward in each moment of your life. The truth will become clear. When you get out of your own way, your life will flow and you will shine!

PRESCRIPTION: WRITE A LETTER TO YOUR FEARS

An important step towards embracing goals which are aligned with your passionate purpose is to move beyond your fears and doubts. Use this exercise to explore, address and push through these hazardous emotions. Complete this letter to your fears and break up with your self-doubt, criticisms and judgments for good!

Dear Fear,

I want to write you this letter. I know in the past I have invited you into my life to try to protect me and help me cope with life's challenges, but I am ready to let you go for good. You are no longer welcome in my life.

Up until this time, I have called on you when:

_____

_____

_____

Reflect on how fear has served you in the past.

You have created a false sense of safety through:

_____

_____

_____

But you have also created chaos and havoc and lead to unhealthy behaviors and thoughts such as:

_____

_____

which have kept me from living my passionate purpose and reaching goals which are truly aligned with my inner light.

Describe some behaviors and sabotaging thoughts based out of fear that you have experienced such as intoxicating yourself with food or alcohol, angry outbursts, shopping addiction, staying overly busy as a distraction, etc. How has fear hurt your progress towards your goals, kept you stuck and held you back from living your authentic purpose?

I am ready to step into my true heart-centered power and move toward goals which are aligned with my authentic self and not distorted by you, my self-doubts, my negative thinking or my destructive behaviors. I choose to create a new experience in my life. I will live from a place of:

_____

I am strong, centered and grounded in my soul truth. I cultivate abundance and joy as I move through my life with ease and grace. If you try to intrude into my life in the future, I will:

_____

_____

Describe how you will deal with fear and the situations, emotions and thoughts that lead to fear-based behaviors in the future. What positive coping mechanisms will you use to keep yourself grounded in your core truth and stop the fear? Perhaps you will envision yourself placing your fears in a bubble when they arise and letting them drift away. Or maybe you will strongly state "stop" or "cancel" each time you sense a fear creeping into your consciousness.

I am moving on and replacing you fear, with faith, trust, grace and:

_____

To my strength and passion!

Signed: _____ Date: _____

Once you complete this letter to release your fear, you can let it go. Try creating a ceremony to let go and say goodbye for good to these limiting thoughts and emotions. You can throw away or burn your letter to release your fears to the universe and end their energy and power over you. You have turned them over to the universe and no longer have to worry about them. You are free!

PRESCRIPTION: GROUNDED, STRONG AND FLEXIBLE TO RIDE OUT THE STORM

True security comes from a sense of being grounded in the present and sure in your talents and faith. As you discover and embrace your highest and most authentic self, you allow essential energy to glow abundantly in your life. When you express the power of grounded peace, you create a calm, trusting energy that radiates out around you. This strength and flexibility allows you to maintain calm order amidst chaos and disorder. You can find stability even with shifting circumstances.

Try the following practice to activate security and tap into your calm, grounded energy. Take the vibrant stability you experience during this exercise into your everyday life. Remember that you can adapt to any situation and remain calm, centered and strong.

Find a quiet place where you will not be disturbed. Sit comfortably and close your eyes. Bring your attention inward. Relax any areas in which you are holding tension. Bring your full awareness to your body, and notice what is there. Settle into a comfortable, relaxed position.

Activate the energy of your root chakra by bringing your breath deep into your pelvis. Breathe in through your nose, and allow the air to flow down into the base of your lungs. Exhale and relax. Feel the stability and groundedness you cultivate with each breath.

Bring your attention to the base of your spine. Feel it root you into the stable, calm energy of the earth. Feel the invincible power of the earth and your connection to her. Feel a clear flow of energy moving into you from the earth, giving you strength and stability.

Feel yourself rooted into the earth like a mighty tree. Sense deep roots connecting into the ground. Allow an unwavering energy to stabilize you and disperse all fears, worries and insecurities. Feel your inner strength growing and radiating all around you to protect you from destabilizing forces.

Allow this stability to give you strength and adaptability to weather any storm. Know that you can adapt to accommodate any demand while remaining flexible yet resilient. Tap into the energy of the tree, the earth and the wind. Feel this unshakable energy fill you, ground you and give you a sense of peace.

Now think of a time when you have faced a challenge with the adaptable strength of this tree. Describe how your breathing, posture and muscles react to taking such an approach. Remember this place of grounded security and strength.

- How did you meet this trial with an invincible yet supple energy?
- What was it like to cultivate this strength and security?
- How did it feel in your body, heart and mind when you were adaptable and confident?

Remember a time when you were a sensible voice of reason in a chaotic situation. Reflect on how it felt when you experienced this calm, balanced strength.

- When were you able to serve as a model of support, grace and security for others?
- How did you cultivate balanced strength to calm others amidst confusion?
- What did you do and say to help others remain grounded?

Feel the memories and sensations you experience when you act from a place of centered security. Realize that you can access this state at any time and settle into the rational, sensible mind whenever you choose, regardless of your environment or the chaos around you. As you manifest peaceful self-expression, you harness true inner strength. This allows you to express your power in a grounded, calming manner. From this place you can find inner peace while supporting others as well.

When you are ready, allow your awareness to broaden. Take some deep breaths and slowly come back to your surroundings. Take the time that you need. As you are ready, open your eyes. Feeling refreshed as you return to your day with a renewed sense of appreciation for all that you have and all that you are. Know that you can tap into this flexible strength and security at any time. You have an invincible power within you!

PRESCRIPTION: TRAIN YOUR BRAIN TO BREAK FREE FROM WORRY

We can become preoccupied with worst-case scenarios and spiral into an endless trail of "what-ifs" if we allow our minds to develop a mental habit of worry. Unrelenting doubts and worries can become paralyzing and sap your emotional energy. As your anxiety levels soar, they can interfere with your forward growth and daily tasks.

Chronic worrying can become a habit that distracts you from your passionate purpose. Fortunately, you can take steps to train your brain to remain calm and take a more positive perspective.

Often when you try to banish worry, it backfires and leads to focusing even more attention on the very thoughts you are trying to diminish. Our brains have a way of jumping to focus on something when we are striving to avoid such thoughts. Instead, it can be helpful to allow yourself permission to have thoughts about the situations you worry about but in a more structured manner so that those thoughts are not allowed to spiral out of control.

Try creating a "worry period." Select a time and place where you give yourself permission each day to empty your mind of your worries. During that "worry period" you are allowed to worry about whatever is on your mind, but the rest of the day your mind remains worry-free. If you begin to experience fear or anxieties during the day, make a note and postpone focusing on that issue until your worry period. Remind yourself that there is no need to dwell on that worry at that time and that you can save it for later while you move on with your day.

During your worry period, review the list of anxieties which you collected during that day, address them and then move on. Deal with each concern on your list, and evaluate the nature of your fears. Ask yourself if each situation is something you are currently experiencing or an imaginary what-if or projection about the future.

Determine if the problem is realistic and if you can do something reasonable to prevent or prepare for it or if it is something that is out of your realm of control. If the problem is something you can solve, determine some specific action steps you can take at this time. Brainstorm specific solutions you can think of, but do not get fixated on finding the perfect resolution. Evaluate your options, and craft an action plan. Start with the first step to deal with the situation.

For unsolvable issues, let go of these worries. Choose to focus on those situations you can change instead of getting caught up in circumstances beyond your control.

Think about how you tend to perceive the world and what worrying provides for you. Reflect on the following questions to develop a better understanding of the way that you deal with uncertainty.

- What evidence do you have that a thought is true? What suggests that it is not true?
- Can everything in life be certain?
- How is a need for certainty helpful? How is it limiting?
- Is there a more constructive, realistic way to view this situation?
- What is the likelihood that what you fear will actually occur? What are some likely outcomes?
- Can you deal with the fear of uncertainty in a more constructive way?
- How does worrying about the situation help you? How does this cycle of fear hurt you?
- What would you say to a friend or loved one who had this concern or worry?

Once you have developed a deeper insight into your patterns of worry and future projection, you can begin to cultivate a greater mindfulness of the present moment. As you are more easily able to ground yourself in the security of the present, you can break free of your worries. Learning to focus your attention in the present moment allows you to let go of fears of what might happen in the future.

Observe your thoughts, and let go of your fears. Acknowledge your anxious feelings and thoughts without trying to suppress them, fight them or ignore them. Simply see that they are present without reacting to them. Allow them to pass by like clouds in the sky. Choose to let go of your fears instead of engaging and becoming stuck. Pay attention to the present moment, your breath and the thoughts drifting in and out of your mind. Notice that you can sit in the stillness that is in the present moment. Each time you consciously choose to remain calm in the flow of the present, you reinforce a positive habit that will help you break free of the negative cycle of worry and fear over time.

These practices can help you break the habit of dwelling on worries and help you remain calm in the present moment. You will begin to realize that you have more control over your thoughts then you previously recognized.

CHAPTER 12: Settle Into Your True Essence of Inner Joy

FREQUENTLY, THE QUEST for happiness can seem like an endless pursuit. You may think to yourself, "I'll be happier when…" When I get a promotion. When I conquer that fear. When I am in better shape. When I feel more energetic. This pursuit of happiness strives for outside promises to give you satisfaction in some longed for future.

But in reality, happiness is not an aspiration or something you cultivate only once you achieve something you desire. Instead, true happiness stems from within. It is not something you need to seek but instead something which you are. When you are in touch with that essential nature, every experience is infused with joy.

Often, we wait for happiness to come to us. You may search for joy outside of yourself in the form of places, people and things. When you conceive of love as something you lack, you can feel insecure, anxious and fearful.

"Happiness is the spiritual experience of living every minute with love, grace, and gratitude."
-Denis Waitley

In truth, happiness does not come from outside of us. It is not cultivated from relationships, possessions or career success. Instead, happiness is your true nature. Indisputable happiness is an inner contentment and knowledge that things are well. It fills you with a sense of peace and ease, no matter what it going on around you.

Discovering the Source of True Bliss Within

Experiencing joy and connecting with a sense that you are part of something larger than yourself on an everyday basis brings true meaning to your life and makes you feel vibrantly alive. Cultivating this ability to remain in a state of presence and appreciate ordinary beauty and everyday miracles adds wonder to each day which fills your life with meaning and purpose.

We often search for happiness outside of ourselves—in a dream career, a perfect body, an ideal relationship, a joyous family. Yet this quest for outward satisfaction sets us on an erroneous mission in which we are searching for something more based on false projections. This misguided pursuit keeps us constantly busy, struggling to achieve more, build more wealth and collect more friends. We are overwhelmed with doing and achieving as we chase external satisfaction.

Yet the truth is that happiness is a choice. Every moment presents the opportunity for experiencing joy. Remain open to abundance, opportunities and pleasure. True happiness lies within you. There is nothing out there that can satisfy that emptiness or bring you that sought-after peace.

As you recognize that real happiness evolves from a sense of wholeness and self-knowing, you awaken to the experience of completeness that arises from embracing your true self. You have all possibilities within you. This sense of totality brings contentment as you do not feel a lack of any kind. From this place, everything is fine just as it is.

You must develop a rich inner awareness to shift away from a relentless chase of outside pleasures and external acknowledgement to reconnect with your essential truth. You must find a stillness to hear your inner knowledge and loving presence. Once you shift your perspective, you can recognize the wholeness that is already yours.

"The amount of happiness that you have depends on the amount of freedom you have in your heart."
-Thich Nhat Hanh

Great spiritual traditions and modern science alike show us that the human soul and brain can generate happiness. You have within you the power and capacity to choose your experience. When you choose to focus on positive thoughts and actions, you change your brain's biochemistry and support the experience of joy. You can tap into the innate joy of your inner spirit without the need for external influences or validation.

Your joy is already within you, arising from your authentic core self. As you align with this essential essence of your being, you tap into the source of all joy, inspiration, creativity, intuition and purpose. When you deepen your connection to and understanding of your passionate purpose and true path, you open your heart and mind to allow yourself to embrace your vital spirit.

As you make this choice of true happiness and authentic inner satisfaction over delusional fear, struggle and overwhelm, you will retrain yourself to pay attention to your inner perceptions, desires and emotions. Repeating this new pattern and living from a more authentic spirit literally changes your mind. The neural pathways in your brain rewire and subtle shifts settle in, bringing you a sense of joy and ease of life that you will never achieve from reaching for outside satisfaction.

While external happiness fades with time, the source of happiness within you is permanent. As you open to greater possibilities and connect with a sense of what really matters, you can find a more profound sense of happiness which is all around you. This essential happiness is not a goal but a knowing which you have inside you. It is at the core of who you are. It is within you. It is your true essence.

Settling Into Your Natural Joy and Connecting with Love

"Happiness is the absence of striving for happiness."
-Chuang Tzu

Acknowledging that love is always with you in your essential nature reminds you that you have a full loving heart with you at all times. As you open your heart to the internal flow of joy and awareness that connects you to everything in creation, fear, uncertainty and unease melt away. You open a space and stillness for inner peace that no one can take away from you.

This feeling of true love as something which you are within the core of your essence shifts the way you relate to yourself and to other people in the world. Knowing that you are fundamentally love allows you to simply express love with unconditional generosity. This state of pure love creates connections that fill your heart with joy.

When you are living from your truest essence, you open yourself up to deeper possibilities. The mind and ego tend to distort your experience of reality. They may create false stories that can hold you back from your true intentions. The more you can examine the stories you tell yourself and the ego-based delusions that warp your inner dialogue, the easier it is to settle into your natural joy and connect with your essential nature of love.

Exploring the type of story you want to tell and shifting to a narrative fostered out of love leads you to rediscover compassion and truth. You are able to shift your narrative, forgive yourself and others and choose the next steps to take back your power and create any experience you desire. This creates the possibility of limitless joy and love.

As you reconnect with that essential source and open the flow of this joyful energy that you have within, you can experience authentic pleasure at its fullest. In this state you are living a life that is aligned with your passionate purpose. You are able to express your genuine magnificence. In this state, you are open to inspiration and insight.

Happiness already exists with you. This joy is able to grow and shine forth when you pause to experience the present moment. Embrace your existence with gratitude, compassion and awe. When you are aligned with this state, every choice you make will support the expansion of this joy, and life keeps getting better and better!

The natural expression of our happiness is to serve others in the world. As you act from the core of your authentic soul and carry out your passionate purpose, happiness expands within you and spreads out from you into the world. Once you are connected to your true essence, you uncover understanding, fulfillment and joy in all of your actions.

Assisting others who are struggling with similar obstacles which you have encountered along your path can help deepen your inner peace and uncover boundless joy. When you selflessly serve others, something powerful occurs. You unblock barriers to more profound contentment. As you amplify your own happiness, you express more of your true nature. Joy expands out from within you into the world like a seed budding forth.

You do not have to strive for this love and happiness because they are already part of your essential nature. As you settle into a calm stillness, you can tap into that joy and bliss which is within you, waiting to be nurtured and expanded. Your thoughts and actions can either contribute to or detract from this inner rapture and delight. The most powerful input comes from the deepest level of your awareness when you are acting in alignment with your authentic self. Happiness can then expand and permeate mind and body and trickle out into the world.

As you release judgments, doubt and fear you can open to this place of true contentment. Cultivating this awareness will allow you to find that there is no limit to your happiness. As you foster this authentic joy, you will naturally find yourself sharing it with others. This genuine pleasure is consistent and does not depend on the ups and downs of everyday life. You are the source of such permanent and unlimited bliss!

"Find ecstasy in life; the mere sense of living is joy enough."
-Emily Dickinson

Create a Life From Which You Do Not Need to Escape

When you overcome fear and step into your authentic confidence, you can choose to follow your intuition and fulfil your true passionate purpose! Sometimes, fear of failure can hold you back from the life you are meant to live. You yearn to fulfil your dreams and uphold your soul's passionate calling, but it may seem simpler to hold back and take the "easier" or more obvious path.

When you back away from your deepest calling and settle for a mediocre life, you are constantly chasing something more. You work harder and harder, spend more time at the office, collect more and more possessions, and yet you never feel truly fulfilled. You may dread Mondays, count down the minutes until the end of the day and tick off boxes on the calendar until you can get away from it all. You are running away from your life as it currently exists.

The key to fulfillment and peace lies in creating and living a life from which you do not need to escape! The path that leads to true fulfillment is already laid out, and you hold the map. Deep within you, you know your authentic calling. You understand all those things you have always wanted to do. You comprehend the larger purpose that is beckoning you to bring it to fruition. When you embrace a confident spirit, take a leap of faith and follow your dreams, you create a life that feeds your soul!

This allows you to create a reality you truly love and believe in and permits you to renew yourself daily. You become refreshed and revitalized each day. You are filled with inspiration and vision for creating infinite possibilities. To do this, you must rest in the present moment. As you release past disappointments and future fears, you are free to create true joy in your present experience.

As you take a leap of faith and trust the guidance of your soul, you will find a sense of peace and true happiness. When you live your dreams in alignment with your greater passionate purpose, life flows more easily. You no longer need to continuously search for happiness in outside sources—in friendships, possessions, relationships, material things, careers and external feedback. Instead of grasping at the next quick fix to make you feel good temporarily, you create lasting satisfaction.

Embracing your dreams without fear of failure leads to the ability to confront life as the happiest version of yourself. Once you tap into that deep sense of harmony and stop relying on others for happiness, you will find true joy in its purest form within you. You already have all that you need. Connecting with and accepting your full and authentic self allows you to dream bigger and reach your full potential!

PRESCRIPTION: STOP AND SMELL THE FLOWERS

Nature can soothe us, bring us a profound sense of peace and joy and help ground us in the present moment. As you become caught up in the busyness of modern life, rushing around from one responsibility to the next, you may find yourself disconnected from the rhythms of nature.

Yet nature offers immense comfort when we take the time to appreciate and connect with her. Use this prescription to make an effort to get reacquainted with nature, and enhance your connection with life around you. Through time spent in nature, you will find that you can awaken, ease into your body, boost creativity and find a greater quality of life.

Try some of these suggestions for cultivating a greater awareness and connection with the natural world. Notice how this facilitates a sense of peace and stillness from which you are better able to connect with yourself as well.

Stop and Smell the Flowers

When was the last time you paused to smell a blooming flower or truly listen to the birds singing at dawn? Just as slowing down to savor each bite of your meal helps you more fully acknowledge what you are eating, practicing mindfulness in other ways can also cultivate a more profound sense of wellbeing. Taking time to pause and appreciate the beauty that nature provides can help you develop a sense of gratitude and mindfulness that will build joy. As you notice all the beauty in the world, you find more and more things to be grateful for which further enhances your overall joy in life.

Explore the World Around You

Remember when you were a child, and you could spend hours exploring every aspect of a tree or enjoy an entire day basking in the joy of the beach? Most children are innately curious and naturally explore the world around them. They look at the world as a gift to be explored and enjoyed. As adults, too often we forget this perspective of curiosity. You can become so set in your busy routine and normal way of doing things that you forget the joy of discovering new corners of the world, appreciating little pleasures and delighting in new ways of doing things. Happiness can be found in the joy of the moment. Take a chance this week to explore new things and create joyful moments. Try a new restaurant, take a new route or hike a different path. Explore the world around you, and discover all that it has to offer.

Play in the Dirt

Touching the earth can be a profound way to become more deeply connected with nature and therefore yourself. Notice what occurs when you take time to make contact with the earth. Go outside, take off your shoes and walk in the sand or grass. Find a tree and place your palms on the trunk. It can also be energizing to dig in the garden, grow your own herbs, keep house plants or play in the sand. Notice the feeling of reaching out and touching nature. Feel the sense of love, joy and connection to that which is beyond yourself.

PRESCRIPTION: INSPIRE HAPPINESS

Finding and creating inspiration for manifesting greater happiness in your life can take many forms. Explore some of the following areas and values. Notice what speaks to you and empowers you to connect with your inner essential joy.

Think about your deepest longings. Your true desires are cues that lead you to authentic happiness, delight and creativity. As you uncover your deepest yearnings and find the stillness to really listen to your soul's calling, you awaken to your passionate purpose and true path. This brings a sense of wellbeing that surpasses the shifting nature of day-to-day life. This true joy permeates everything that you do. Deepening your connection with your authentic inner life energy allows joy to flow effortlessly in your life.

Notice the way you feel, think, act and express yourself when you make time for and prioritize your passionate purpose. When you are living a life that is aligned with your true desires you exude a genuine joy that is contagious. Embrace your passions, and you will inspire those around you to live a more fulfilled life as well.

- What are you passionate about spending your time doing?
- When you are engaged in your passionate purpose what is it like? How do you feel? How do you relate to the world?
- What inspires you to engage in this pursuit?

Explore various aspects of your life and how you can cultivate and inspire greater happiness through each of those. Develop and journal about resolutions you will work towards related to different elements of your life. Be specific, and set measureable objectives. Think about how these resolutions fit in with your greater passionate purpose and inspire authentic happiness.

- Think about actions and goals related to the following aspects of your life: Attitude, Creativity, Dreams, Health, Family, Fun, Gratitude, Mindfulness, Nourishment, Relationships, Service and Spirituality.

- Find concrete, measureable actions that you will take to bring about these changes.
- Decide how you will hold yourself accountable for keeping these pledges.

After one month, revisit your objectives in each area. Reflect on how often you acted in alignment with your intentions in each realm.

- If you made progress towards your resolutions, did it make you happier? In what way(s)?
- If you did not stick to your objectives, what got in your way?

Revisit your goals each month, and note how you are moving towards greater fulfillment of each one. If appropriate, adjust, re-commit or change a resolution that does not feel quite aligned with your overall goals. Notice any adjustments you need to make in order to bring about the shifts you seek.

PRESCRIPTION: UNCOVERING JOY

Happiness is something which is found within. As you slow down and find the stillness to recognize it, you will uncover love, hope, inspiration, peace and joy. Your happiness will blossom and spread into every aspect of your life and the world around you.

Our natural state is one where we live and express our joy. It is innate to convey and share our happiness with others. Unfortunately, we often become scarred by experiences in life, develop fears and create barriers to the natural flow of love in our life. You may become guarded with expressing your emotions and limit the expression of happiness in your life.

Take some time to reconnect with your natural state of joy. Begin to open up to happiness, and allow it to expand into all areas of your life. You are here to appreciate and radiate joy. You can choose happiness in each moment as you connect to that core place of love and joy within you. As you recognize the good in your life, watch how more and more joy permeates each moment. Live your joy. Express happiness and watch it grow.

Reflect on how you experience and convey joy in your life. Expressing joy does not have to be a grand statement or attention grabbing gesture. It can be subtle, nurturing, comforting or simple. It can be as delicate as sharing a smile or spreading laughter.

Think about any areas of your life where you hold yourself back from experiencing and expressing your authentic happiness.

- Are you ready to stop repressing your natural, innate joy?
- What is stopping you from removing hesitation and accepting the flow of happiness in your life?
- Where and how can you commit to allowing more joy into your life?

Encourage yourself to smile, laugh, play and give of yourself with joyful energy. Reflect on how you will allow your inner joy to fully emerge in your life. Think about the familiar things around you which you may be able to rediscover with new eyes. Slow down, find stillness and notice the wonder all around you.

- Recall several aspects of life which bring you joy that you can encourage in your life. How can you build a sense of wonder in your life? What would allow you to experience more joy?
- What allows you to express and experience joy?

Think about people who exude happiness. Note what type of energy they exude.

- Is there something about the way that they react to, relate to and/or experience life's events that you would like to express as well?
- Where in your life do you want to live with joy like that?

Use the insights you discover through these reflections to uncover more joy in your life. Each day, look at the areas of your life where you can nurture happiness and inspire joy!

PRESCRIPTION: PRIORITIZE SELF-CARE

It is important to take care of you and to remember that your needs matter. As you prioritize your self-care and look out for yourself, you enable your essential joy to shine forth even brighter. Taking care of your own needs liberates more energy that allows you to care for and help others as well.

Think about the following aspects of your life, and decide where you would like to focus more of your time and energy. Start doing things for yourself, and watch your happiness grow. As you make time and space for self-care, you can revive habits that serve your well-being and inner growth.

Learn to love yourself first

Self-love and self-care are not narcissistic or selfish concepts. Instead, loving yourself involves welcoming the core authentic person you are meant to be in the world. As you cultivate the gifts and talents which you have, you treat yourself with respect, care and compassion.

Love yourself for who you are. This allows you to take better care of yourself and start making your happiness a priority. Once your needs are met and you are looking out for yourself, you are more likely to be capable of genuinely helping those who also need your compassion, forgiveness and support.

Tapping into the true joy within you, allows you to become a source of uplifting support and happiness which spreads out from you into the world. As others are exposed to your joy, they can open to this positive energy, receive it and amplify it as well. As you love yourself and allow your inner joy to shine forth, you and the world around you will undergo positive transformation!

Embrace your genuine, unique self

A key step in learning to truly love yourself, involves embracing your uniqueness. Discover your strengths, talents, beauty and ideas. Own your authentic self. Be the best version of you on your own terms. Relax and explore your curiosity. Let go and see where playful exploration of your life can take you. Be a bit daring, and try something new that you are drawn to explore. The greatest joys in life often come in unexpected moments. Keep dreaming, exploring and learning as you step into your genuine purpose.

Live in the present

When you are able to slow down and find the stillness amongst the chaos of daily life, your mind and soul can settle into the a place of peace where you will find greater clarity, insight and joy. You can settle into your true essence of love, happiness and awareness. Each moment holds the promise of a miracle. A new beginning. Life is happening now. Stop dwelling in the past or pondering the future. Welcome the present. Experience life as it is happening. Appreciate the beauty that is all around you and within you right now.

Believe in yourself, celebrate small victories and take the next realistic step

When you have the courage to seize the opportunities that come your way, accept challenges and recognize the gifts along your path, you will move forward, knowing you are headed in the right direction. Although every moment does not necessarily seem miraculous, open yourself up to appreciate the small victories in each day. Train yourself to recognize the positive in each situation. Look for happiness and you will find it.

Notice the joy in a cooling breeze, a child's laughter, a smile from a stranger and the small synchronicities in your life. Celebrate these joys in your life. Even when you feel powerless to change a situation, you are able to change how you think about it. Recognize the lessons, the joy and the love you experience along the way.

Consider these guiding principles and reflect on what they mean for you. How can you apply these ideas and values in your life? How does your experience of life change when you remain more aware of these ideas? What does it feel like to prioritize your own happiness? How does this impact your sense of abundance, fulfillment and contentment?

CONCLUSIONS and NEXT STEPS: Move Forward with Authentic Grace, Possibility and Mindful Presence

CONGRATULATIONS ON achieving *The Whole Cure*! As you have worked your way through these fifty-two carefully crafted prescriptions, you have gained a wealth of insight into your authentic self and how to let her shine! Now is the time to put together everything you have learned and been working on. Allow this deepened insight and awareness to support you and lead you to overcome overwhelm, reclaim balance and reconnect with a life you love!

Sometimes life can seem complicated or confusing. There is so much information available to us, and it can be easy to feel a little lost. Thankfully, true wisdom comes from within. You have everything you need already inside of you. As you reconnect with your most genuine self, you gain immense insight. You find a freedom and ease which allows for vast transformation and unlimited possibilities.

"To be beautiful means to be yourself. You don't need to be accepted by others. You need to accept yourself."
-Thich Nhat Hanh

You have a choice to live your life from peace or to become stuck in a downward spiral of doubt, fear and unease. When you are living in fear, you retreat from possibilities, repress your true potential and pull back from life. Instead, when you act from love, you open yourself to all that life offers, you embrace your passionate purpose and you receive joy, acceptance, excitement and delight.

By cultivating greater awareness, you can break through the boundaries imposed by false stories created when your ego and mind control your life experience. Foster a stance of love and truth. As you pattern yourself to respond with greater compassion, grace and awareness, you can forgive yourself for mistakes and take time to rewrite your story.

Compassion is necessary in order for us to experience peace. Peace within ourselves and amongst our communities. It is essential for mental stability, consistent kindness and peaceful presence. This stance allows you to take back your power and step into your full promise. You can create your present and your future. You have a limitless ability to craft any experience you desire and live the life you envision.

To start, it is crucial to love yourself. When you can accept yourself with all of your passion, potential, abilities, talents, gifts, mistakes and imperfections, you can fully cultivate your capacity to express and truly be love. From this state, you open your ability to create, contribute and participate in the world around you. And you free your heart to exude love out into the world. Your ability to love yourself fully frees the love that is your true nature. You can fearlessly embrace your true authentic self and follow your calling as you live fearlessly to create a better world for all.

Now is your time to step into your authentic self. Trust your heart, love your body and be true to yourself. Take action each day to align your behaviors, thoughts, emotions and life with love. Stop hiding from what you truly want in your life and what you have to give to the world. As you love yourself and embrace your passion, you generate an energy of enthusiasm, joy and positivity that spreads into the world.

As you accept the invitation to open to the fullness of life, you choose to shine brilliantly. You no longer need to play small out of fear, doubt or unease. Now is the time to express your love freely and no longer hold back in life. Explore your unique expression, and share your passionate purpose.

Stay flexible. There is no need to resist. *The Whole Cure* is about leaning in, and not struggling against your life. You are connecting with the flow of happiness that gives your life true meaning, purpose and fulfillment. We are happiest and most inspired when our lives have clarity, direction and significance. Your core nature is guiding you in the most essential way. As you listen, life flows, decisions are easy and there is no struggle.

Intuitively, you know the things that nurture you at a deep level. You just need to slow down, listen and pay attention to the signals that are all around you all the time. As you move with the clear flow of life's guidance, your joy expands and you awaken your true self. A clear path of evolution flows before you, and your actions align with joy.

As you accept these carefully crafted prescriptions, you engage in a process which builds your inner awareness and true contentment. Real happiness arises from your core and allows you to know that you have everything you need to feel good right now. Your essential nature is settled, confident and fulfilled, regardless of outside circumstances.

As you become more aware and aligned with this energy, your thoughts, words and behaviors are naturally filled with value and meaning. Your happiness effortlessly expands as you live a dedicated life. Your life and actions have meaning and purpose. This direction gives you satisfaction, pleasure and ease. Create an intention of leading a purposeful life while prioritizing time to take care of yourself.

As humans, we are genetically hardwired to seek and need approval. This works well for us as young children, as we follow rules to keep us safe in order to gain our parents' approval. But as we grow up, we are forced to go out into the world and fend for ourselves. Often, the need for approval from parents is simply replaced with a drive for satisfaction from other outside sources. You may strive for the best education, money, power, fame, relationships, a big home, the most elite career and more as you seek the approval of others.

This drive to mold your behavior to seek outward praise can detract from your true nature. You can become distracted from your genuine loving, joyful and pure spirit. This journey towards *The Whole Cure* has created clarity and ease. You have uncovered your inner strength and stepped into a place where you act based on your true, compassionate, loving and joyful self instead of responding from a place of hurt, overwhelm and fear.

Become clear about your true passions, dreams and purpose. What do you truly want to do with your life when nothing is holding you back? What is your biggest dream and goal that will encourage the expression of your genuine, lasting inner happiness? How can you support yourself to get to your hopes and dreams without feeling restricted, overworked or drained?

When you realize that you have all that you need and that nothing is lacking, life flows effortlessly. You realize that all you desire belongs to you. You remove the extraneous barriers you have created which block the process of receiving your true path.

"Remember, this moment is the only one. The beginning and the end of your experience is the here and now."
-Mirka Kraftsow

As you live effortlessly, you will find that your goals are easier to achieve, love is more abundant and happiness arises from within. You will settle into a freedom that comes with knowing who you are and trusting that wisdom. Closely examine the present you are constructing, and align that reality with the future you dream of!

By aligning your thoughts, words and actions with your true nature you do not need to accomplish anything. You find a deeper awareness that brings greater growth, ease and grace. As you express your true self, you are free and can reconnect with a life you sincerely love!

The Whole Cure provides you with guidance, inspiration and resources to engage your inner awareness in the lifelong process of self-discovery and deepening your connection with what is really most important to you. These prescriptions help you cultivate the kind of presence that allows you to move in new directions and find fresh approaches to evoking true joy and satisfaction. You have the possibilities to help you get there. Put these concepts into practice one at a time, come back to the ones that are calling you or try several at once. Whatever approach you choose, you will feel more alive, more present and more aware.

You have cultivated boundless insight and ability to shift your patterns. Through patience, preparation, observation and inspiration, you have sown the seeds of growth and awareness which will continue to self-generate, sustain and renew.

Upgrading your life with *The Whole Cure* gives you a lightness of being and deeper clarity of thought and intuition. Your overall quality of life will be renewed and rejuvenated as you release tension in the mind, body and spirit, let go of negative emotions and quiet the noise that distracts you from true meaning. This enables clear manifestation of your abilities as you are filled with a peaceful flow of love, happiness and energy. You create a life which you love and which truly nourishes you as you remove extraneous things that previously caused life to be more of a struggle.

As you move forward, dream big dreams, explore new things, uncover your deepest passions and be a wellspring of inspiration. Approach the world with an open mind, heart and spirit and make bold choices. Be grateful for the little things along with the big. Laugh often and smile with your whole being. Remember to take time for play, to have fun and to experience the world with fresh eyes. Make the most of each moment, and enjoy the peace and joy that you have within!

A large part of continuing to live an authentic and aligned life is believing in yourself and having adequate support and inspiration. When life inevitably presents challenges or you feel discouraged, remember that you always have the present moment. Settle into a stillness, quiet your mind and connect with your center. Explore that which you choose to focus your energy, time, attention and love on at that instant. This reflection will grant you insight and illuminate your path forward.

Life demands planning, vision, encouragement, connection and insight. If you desire support in discovering your life's path or making your dreams a reality, you can always reach out to me for assistance and guidance. I offer various opportunities to help you take this process and positive momentum further. Explore the ways I can help you reach your goals and achieve optimal health at http://www.JenniferWeinbergMD.com or email me at info@JenniferWeinbergMD.com to figure out your personalized plan for sustainable health and happiness!

Motivation comes from engaging in the process with the proper tools, support and accountability. I am honored to continue to work with you as you commit to moving along the pathway to greater health, balance, fulfillment and satisfaction. This can open doors to a revitalized life and an energized vision. You are an active participant in your future!

About Dr. Jennifer L. Weinberg, MD, MPH, MBE

Dr. Jennifer L. Weinberg, MD, MPH, MBE is a Preventive and Lifestyle Medicine Physician trained at the University of Pennsylvania and Johns Hopkins. As a Consultant, Author, Wellness Expert, Speaker, Interdisciplinary Yoga Instructor, Board Certified Holistic Health Coach, and the founder of The Simple | Pure | Whole™ Wellness Method, Dr. Weinberg is deeply passionate about inspiring others to reclaim a life of ease, vitality and health.

She specializes in empowering individuals to heal themselves and live a pure, whole life through lifestyle, mind-body techniques and decreased toxic environmental exposures. To do so, Dr. Weinberg offers innovative online wellness and education programs for individuals looking for sustainable optimal health as well as health care providers seeking to embrace a transformative approach to health care and corporations wanting to integrate a holistic approach to corporate wellness!

Her methods have helped thousands relieve suffering and regain a fresh perspective and approach to true joy and health! One patient declared her to be "the ultimate teammate on the path to lifelong health!" while another student described her as "an exceptional teacher." Learn more at http://www.JenniferWeinbergMD.com

34187811R00096

Made in the USA
Charleston, SC
03 October 2014